The AA POCKET Guide
MALLORCA

D0726553

Mallorca: Regions and Best places to see

Original text by Tony Kelly
Updated by Mona King

© Automobile Association Developments Limited 2008
First published 2008
Reprinted July 2008

ISBN: 978-0-7495-5522-1

Published by AA Publishing, a trading name of Automobile Association Developments
Limited, whose registered office is Fanum House, Basing View, Basingstoke, Hampshire
RG21 4EA. Registered number 1878835.

Colour separation: Keenes, Andover
Printed and bound in Italy by Printer Trento S.r.l.

Front cover images: (t) AA/P Baker; (b) AA/K Paterson
Back cover image: AA/K Paterson

A03876
Maps in this title produced from mapping © KOMPASS GmbH,
A-6063 Rum, Innsbruck

About this book

Symbols are used to denote the following categories:

✚ map reference

✉ address or location

☎ telephone number

🕒 opening times

💷 admission charge

🍴 restaurant or café on premises
   or nearby

🚇 nearest underground train station

🚌 nearest bus/tram route

🚆 nearest overground train station

⛴ nearest ferry stop

ℹ tourist information office

❓ other practical information

⬌ other places of interest nearby

▶ indicates the page where you will
   find a fuller description

This book is divided into four sections.

Planning pages 6–19
Before You Go; Getting There; Getting
Around; Being There

Best places to see pages 20–41
The unmissable highlights of any visit
to Mallorca

Exploring pages 42–126
The best places to visit in Mallorca,
organized by area

Maps pages 131–144
All map references are to the atlas
section. For example, Alcúdia has the
reference ✚ 134 C3 – indicating the
page number and grid square in which it
is to be found

Contents

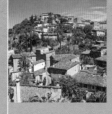

Planning

Before You Go

WHEN TO GO

	JAN	FEB	MAR	APR	MAY	JUN	JUL	AUG	SEP	OCT	NOV	DEC
	14°C	15°C	17°C	19°C	22°C	26°C	29°C	29°C	27°C	23°C	18°C	15°C
	57°F	59°F	63°F	66°F	72°F	79°F	84°F	84°F	81°F	73°F	64°F	59°F

 High season   Low season

The above temperatures are the average daily maximum for each month. Minimum temperatures can often be very much lower than this. They may drop to as little as 2 or 3°C (35 or 37°F) during January and February, but they seldom drop below 20°C (68°F) in July and August.

Sunshine is almost guaranteed throughout the summer, which is the peak tourist season. If you want to avoid the crowds come during May, June, September or October.

Many resorts close during the winter, and this may be a good time to take a city break in Palma or a walking or golfing holiday. During winter it may still be warm enough to eat outside, but bring suitable clothes for cool evenings, particularly in the mountains.

WHAT YOU NEED

● Required   ○ Suggested   ▲ Not required

Some countries require a passport to remain valid for a minimum period (usually at least six months) beyond the date of entry – contact their consulate or embassy or your travel agent for details.

	UK	Germany	USA	Netherlands	Spain
Passport (or National Identity Card where applicable)	●	●	●	●	▲
Visa (regulations can change – check before you travel)	▲	▲	▲	▲	▲
Onward or Return Ticket	○	○	●	○	○
Health Inoculations (tetanus and polio)	▲	▲	▲	▲	▲
Health Documentation (➤ 9, Health advice)	●	●	●	●	▲
Travel Insurance	○	○	○	○	○
Driving Licence (national)	●	●	●	●	●
Car Insurance Certificate	●	●	●	●	○
Car Registration Document	●	●	●	●	○

ADVANCE PLANNING
WEBSITES
● **www.**tourspain.co.uk (Spanish National Tourist Office)
● **www.**majorca-mallorca.co.uk (useful information on all the main resorts)
● **www.**okspain.org (official website for the Tourist Office of Spain)
● **www.**spain.info (official website for Tourism in Spain)
● **www.**digitalmajorca.com (Mallorca/Majorca tourist information site)

TOURIST OFFICES AT HOME
In the UK
Spanish Tourist Office ✉ PO Box 4009, London W1A 6NB ☎ 0207 486 8077

In the USA
Tourist Office of Spain ✉ 666 Fifth Avenue 35th, New York, NY 10103 ☎ 212/265-8822

Tourist Office of Spain ✉ 1395 Brickell Avenue, Suite 1130, Miami, FL 33131 ☎ 305/358-1992

HEALTH ADVICE
Insurance Nationals of EU and certain other countries can get medical treatment in Spain with the relevant documentation (European Health Insurance Card/EHIC), although private medical insurance is still advised and is essential for all other visitors.

Dental services Dental treatment is not usually available free of charge as all dentists practise privately. A list of *dentistas* can be found in the yellow pages of the telephone directory. Dental treatment should be covered by private medical insurance.

TIME DIFFERENCES

GMT	Mallorca	Germany	USA (NY)	Netherlands	Rest of Spain
12 noon	1PM	1PM	7AM	1PM	1PM

Like the rest of Spain, Mallorca is one hour ahead of Greenwich Mean Time (GMT+1), but from late March until late October, summer time (GMT+2) operates. The Spanish attitude to time is much more laid-back than in northern Europe.

WHAT'S ON WHEN

January *Cabalgata de los Reyes Magos* (5 Jan): The Three Kings arrive by boat in Palma to distribute gifts to the city's children.
Sant Antoni Abat (16–17 Jan): Processions of pets and farm animals in Palma, Artà and Sa Pobla.
Sant Sebastià (19 Jan): Bonfires and barbecues in Palma's squares.

February *Sa Rúa* (final weekend before Lent): Carnival held in Palma and elsewhere on the last weekend before Lent. It is marked by bonfires, fancy dress and processions of decorated floats. In Montuïri the Carnival is known as *els darres dies* (the last days).

March/April *Semana Santa* (Holy Week): A week of solemn Easter preparation begins on Palm Sunday, when palm and olive branches are blessed at churches across the island before being taken home to adorn front doors. During Holy Week there are processions every day in Palma; the biggest procession is on Maundy Thursday. Other towns and villages have their own processions too. On the evening of Good Friday a figure of Christ is lowered from his cross in Pollença and carried down the

Calvary steps in silence. A similar event takes place on the church steps in Felanitx.

May *Moros i Cristians* (8–10 May): Mock battles between heroes and infidels in Sóller, commemorating a 1561 battle in which local women helped to defeat a band of Turkish pirates.

June *Sant Pere* (28–29 Jun): Processions of fishing boats in Palma, Port d'Andratx and Port d'Alcúdia in honour of the patron saint of fishermen.

July *La Virgen del Carmen* (16 Jul): Processions of boats in the island's ports, including Cala Rajada, Port de Pollença and Port de Sóller.

NATIONAL HOLIDAYS

JAN	FEB	MAR	APR	MAY	JUN	JUL	AUG	SEP	OCT	NOV	DEC
2		(2)	(2)	1			1		1	1	3

1 January	New Year's Day
6 January	Epiphany
March/April	Good Friday and Easter Monday
1 May	Labour Day
15 August	Assumption of the Virgin
12 October	National Day
1 November	All Saints' Day
6 December	Constitution Day
8 December	Feast of the Immaculate Conception
25 December	Christmas Day

Many shops and offices close for longer periods around Christmas and Easter, as well as for the festivals of Corpus Christi in May/June and Sant Jaume on 25 July

Santa Catalina Thomás (27–28 Jul): Homage to Mallorca's patron saint in her home town of Valldemossa.

August *Sant Bartomeu* (24 Aug): Devil-dancing in Montuïri at one of Mallorca's oldest festivals.
Sant Agusti (28 Aug): *Cavallets* dances in Felanitx, with children dressed as cardboard horses being chased by giants to the accompaniment of bagpipes, flutes and drums.

September/October
Harvest festivals including a melon festival in Vilafranca de Bonany (second Sun in Sep), a wine fair in Binissalem (last Sun in Sep) and a *botifarró* (blood sausage) festival in Sant Joan (third Sun in Oct).

December *Festa de l'Estendard* (31 Dec): Palma commemorates the anniversary of the Christian conquest with a procession from the town hall to Mass at the cathedral.

Mallorcan Festivals
Most traditional *festas* are religious in origin and a few date back to the time of the Christian conquest. Every town and village has its saint's day, whose eve *(revelta)* is marked by a *verbena*, a street party with music, dancing, fireworks and fancy dress. Battles are acted out between devils and heroic women, or Christians and Moors; people prance about as horses, and a good time is had by all.

Getting There

BY AIR

Palma's Son Sant Joan Airport (☎ 971 789000/789099; **www.**aena.es), about 11km (7 miles) east of Palma city centre, is where most people first arrive in Mallorca. The aiport began as a provincial airport and has grown to become one of the busiest in Europe during the peak summer months of June to September, handling more than 20 million passengers each year.

The main terminal is surprisingly spread out and the baggage handling area is quite a way from the flight gates; it can be up to a 30-minute walk from some gates to the baggage area, but there are some moving walkways.

Son Sant Joan has all the amenities of a modern airport including an information desk and tourist information office on the ground floor. There are plenty of ATMs and a café and newsagent, all on the ground floor, and a post office is situated on the second floor. The pre-departure lounge on the fourth floor has a good range of shops selling wines and spirits, food, jewellery and electronic equipment, as well as a branch of La Caixa bank and a pharmacy.

AIRPORT TRANSFERS

Outside the airport there are plenty of taxis 24 hours a day, but they are expensive. In the arrivals hall of the airport there is a price list of standard journeys around the island where you can check your fare before you take the taxi.

BUSES

The No 1 bus runs from the airport (6am–2.15am daily) to Palma via the Plaça d'Espanya and then on along the seafront to the maritime station and port. At the Plaça d'Espanya you can catch trains and other buses for destinations around the island.

ARRIVING BY SEA

Although most visitors fly into Mallorca, up to a million still arrive by sea on the many cruise ships that ply the Mediterranean waters and the ferries that cross to the island from mainland Spain and the other outlying islands. They dock in Palma harbour, but the car and passsenger ferries from Menorca, Barcelona, Ibiza and Valencia dock at the commercial port at Palma.

From the port you can catch the No 1 bus into Palma, from where you can connect with transport to get around the island.

Getting Around

PUBLIC TRANSPORT

TRAINS

The main railway line connects
Palma to Inca, with branch lines to
Sa Pobla (via Muro) and Manacor
(via Sineu and Petra). There are
regular trains throughout the day,
taking around 35 minutes to Inca
and 1 hour to Manacor (☎ 971
752245). Five trains a day leave
Palma for Sóller, beginning at 8am
(☎ 971 752051) and connecting
with the tram to Port de Sóller
(➤ 82–83). The two railway

stations are found close together in
Palma, beside Plaça d'Espanya.

BUSES

A comprehensive network of buses
connects Palma to Mallorca's main
towns, with extra services linking
the coastal resorts in summer.
Buses out of Palma depart from
the bus station on Carrer Eusebi
Estada, behind Plaça d'Espanya.
Palma has its own network of city
buses, which also covers the beach
resorts around Palma Bay (☎ 971
214444). Bus No 1 runs from 6am

to 2am between the airport, city centre and port.

BOAT TRIPS

In summer there are regular boat tours of Palma Bay and excursions from resorts including Cala d'Or, Port de Pollença and Port de Sóller. Some go to remote beaches which can only be reached by boat. There is also the day trip to Cabrera (▶ 103). One trip which runs throughout the year is the journey around the northwest coast from Port de Sóller to Sa Colobra (☎ 971 630170).

MENORCA

Day trips to Menorca can be made on a fast catamaran, which leaves Cala Rajada at 9am daily, arriving at the Menorcan city of Ciutadella in one hour. The return journey leaves Ciutadella at 7.30pm (Cape Balear ☎ 902 100444). There are also daily car ferries to Ciutadella from Port d'Alcúdia (☎ 902 119128).

CAR RENTAL

The leading international car rental companies have offices at Palma airport and you can reserve a car in advance (essential in peak periods) either direct or through a travel agent. Local companies offer competitive rates and will usually deliver a car to the airport.

If the rental car you are driving breaks down follow the instructions given in the documentation; most of the international rental firms provide a rescue service.

TAXIS

Taxis can be hired at ranks (indicated by a blue square with a 'T'), on the street (by flagging down those with a green light) or at hotels. They are good value within Palma but expensive over long

distances. A list of tariffs is displayed at taxi ranks.

CONCESSIONS

Students Holders of an International Student Identity Card may be able to obtain some concessions on travel, entrance fees etc, but Mallorca is not really geared up for students, it is more suited to families and senior citizens. However, there are two youth hostels on the island, one near Palma and the other outside Alcúdia. Another cheap form of accommodation is to stay in a monastery; just turn up or book ahead.

Senior citizens Mallorca is an excellent destination for older travellers, especially in winter when the resorts are quieter, prices more reasonable and hotels offer very economical long-stay rates. The best deals are available through tour operators who specialize in holidays for senior citizens.

DRIVING

Drive on the right.

Speed limits on motorways *(autopistas)*: **120kph (74mph)**
Speed limits on dual carriageways: **100kph (62mph)**
Speed limits on major roads: **90kph (56mph)**
Speed limits on urban roads: **50kph (31mph)**

Seat belts must be worn at all times. Children under 12 must use a child seat.

Random breath-testing takes place. Never drive under the influence of alcohol.

All rental cars take either unleaded petrol *(sin plomo)* or diesel *(gasoleo)*. The top grade is *Super Plus* (98-octane), though *Super* (96-octane) is usually acceptable. Petrol stations are normally open 6am–10pm, and closed Sundays, though larger ones (often self service) are open 24 hours. Most take credit cards. Note: there are few petrol stations in the mountain areas, so make sure you fill up.

Being There

LOCAL TOURIST OFFICES
(Oficinas de Información Turística – OIT)

Palma
✉ Plaça de la Reina 2, Palma 07012 ☎ 971 712216
✉ Ca'n Solleric, Passeig des Born 27, Palma 07001 ☎ 971 724090
✉ Parc de les Estacions, Palma 07002 ☎ 971 754329

Palma Nova
✉ Passeig de la Mar 13, Calvià 07181 ☎ 971 682365

Port d'Alcúdia
✉ Passeig Marítim 68, Alcúdia 07410 ☎ 971 547257

Port de Pollença
✉ Carrer de les Monges 9, Pollença 07470 ☎ 971 865467

Sóller
✉ Plaça d'Espanya, Sóller 07100 ☎ 971 638008

Other offices include: Cala d'Or, Cala Millor, Cala Rajada, Cala Sant Vicenç, Ca'n Picafort, Colònia de Sant Jordi, Magaluf, Peguera, Platja de Muro, Port de Sóller, Porto Cristo, S'Arenal, Ses Illetes and Santa Ponça.

CONSULATES
UK ☎ (971) 712445
Germany ☎ (971) 707737
USA ☎ (971) 403707
Netherlands ☎ (971) 716493

TELEPHONES
Most public telephones accept coins, credit cards and telephone cards *(tarjetas telefónicas)*, available from post offices, news kiosks and tobacconists. Instructions are printed in English.

All telephone numbers in Spain have 9 digits. Telephone numbers in Mallorca begin with 971; you must dial all nine digits wherever you are calling from.

To call Mallorca from the UK dial 00 34; from the USA dial 011 34. To call the operator dial 002.

Using the telephone in your hotel room is considerably more

OPENING HOURS

- Shops
- Offices
- Banks
- Churches
- Museums
- Pharmacies

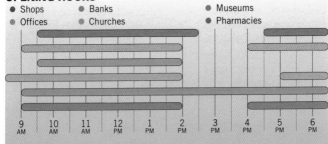

Large department stores, super-markets and shops in tourist resorts may open outside the times shown above, especially in summer. In general, pharmacies, banks and shops close on Saturday afternoon.

Banks close all day Saturday, June to September, but stay open until 4pm Monday to Thursday, October to May.

The opening times of museums is just a rough guide; some are open longer hours in summer while hours are reduced in winter. Some museums close at weekends or another day in the week.

expensive than using a public telephone outside.

INTERNATIONAL DIALLING CODES

From Mallorca (Spain) to:
UK: 00 44
Germany: 00 49
USA: 00 1
Netherlands: 00 31

EMERGENCY TELEPHONE NUMBERS

Police (Policía Local) 092
Police (Policía Nacional) 091
Fire (Bomberos) 080
Ambulance (Ambulància) 061
In any emergency dial 112

POSTAL SERVICES

Post offices are generally open Monday to Friday, 9am–2pm, but some also open in the afternoon and on Saturday morning.

The main post office in Palma at Carrer de Constitució 5 is open Monday to Friday 8.30am to 8.30pm and Saturday 9am–2pm (☎ 902 197197).

Post boxes are bright yellow.

ELECTRICITY

The power supply in Mallorca is: 220–22 volts. Sockets accept two-round-pin-style plugs, so an adaptor is needed for most non-Continental appliances and a transformer for appliances operating on 100–120 volts.

CURRENCY AND EXCHANGE

The euro (€) is the official currency of Spain. Banknotes are in denominations of 5, 10, 20, 50, 100, 200 and 500 euros; coins are in denominations of 1, 2, 5, 10, 20 and 50 cents, and 1 and 2 euros.

Euro traveller's cheques are widely accepted, as are major credit cards. Credit and debit cards can also be used for withdrawing euro notes from cashpoint machines.

HEALTH AND SAFETY

Sun advice The sunniest (and hottest) months are July and August, with an average of 11 hours sun a day and daytime temperatures of 29°C (84°F). During these months particularly you should avoid the midday sun and use a strong sunblock.

Drugs Prescription and non-prescription drugs and medicines are available from pharmacies (*farmàcias*), distinguished by a large green cross. They are able to dispense many drugs which would be available only on prescription in other countries.

Safe water Tap water is generally safe though it can be heavily chlorinated. Mineral water is cheap to buy and is sold as *con gas* (carbonated) and *sin gas* (still). Drink plenty of water during hot weather.

TIPS/GRATUITIES

Yes ✓ No ✗		
Restaurants (if service not included)	✓	10%
Cafés/bars (if service not included)	✓	change
Taxis	✓	10%
Porters	✓	€1
Chambermaids	✓	€1
Cloakroom attendants	✓	change
Hairdressers	✓	change
Theatre/cinema usherettes	✓	change
Toilets	✗	

MEDIA

To find out what's on while you are staying, ask any tourist office for a copy of *Where To Go*, published quarterly in English and German. The *Majorca Daily Bulletin* also has daily listings. A monthly guide to events in Palma is published in Spanish and Catalan and available at tourist offices and hotels.

Remember that everything starts late in Mallorca – opera at 9pm, theatre around 10pm and music any time up to midnight.

PHOTOGRAPHY

What to photograph: mountains, hilltop monasteries, pretty mountain villages and attractive harbours.

Best time to photograph: the Mallorcan summer sun can be powerful at the height of the day making photos taken at this time appear 'flat'; it is best to photograph in the early morning or late evening.

For traditional film-loaded cameras: film and camera batteries are readily available from tourist shops and *droguerías* (pharmacies).

CLOTHING SIZES

France	UK	Rest of Europe	USA	
46	36	46	36	
48	38	48	38	
50	40	50	40	
52	42	52	42	
54	44	54	44	Suits
56	46	56	46	
41	7	41	8	
42	7.5	42	8.5	
43	8.5	43	9.5	
44	9.5	44	10.5	
45	10.5	45	11.5	Shoes
46	11	46	12	
37	14.5	37	14.5	
38	15	38	15	
39/40	15.5	39/40	15.5	
41	16	41	16	
42	16.5	42	16.5	Shirts
43	17	43	17	
36	8	34	6	
38	10	36	8	
40	12	38	10	
42	14	40	12	
44	16	42	14	Dresses
46	18	44	16	
38	4.5	38	6	
38	5	38	6.5	
39	5.5	39	7	
39	6	39	7.5	
40	6.5	40	8	Shoes
41	7	41	8.5	

Best places to see

1 Alcúdia

A perfectly restored walled city on the site of a Roman settlement, with remains of Roman houses and an amphitheatre.

Not to be confused with the holiday resort of the same name, which is actually down at Port d'Alcúdia (▶ 96), the old town is a gem of a place, a maze of narrow streets enclosed by carefully restored medieval ramparts. There were Phoenician and Greek settlements here, but the town reached its heyday in the 2nd century BC, when the Roman invaders made it their capital, Pollentia ('power'). Destroyed by Vandals in the 6th century, the town returned to greatness under the Moors, who built *al-kudia* ('the town on the hill'). The walls you see today were added after the Spanish conquest in the 14th century.

You enter the city through one of the two town gates – the Portal del Moll, with two square towers and two palm trees standing guard, is the symbol of Alcúdia. The narrow streets of the old town, especially Carrer d'en Serra, are resonant of Palma's Arab quarter.

A short walk from the parish church of Sant Jaume takes you to three interesting sights, connected by signposted footpaths. Closest to town are the remains of Roman houses at Pollentia, **Ciutat Romà;** near here are the

well-preserved Teatre Romà (Roman amphitheatre) and the Oratori de Santa Anna, one of Mallorca's oldest churches.

After exploring the Roman remains, interpret them at the **Museu Monogràfic de Pollentia** beside the parish church.

➕ 134 C3 🍴 Choice of restaurants and bars (€–€€) 🚌 From Palma/Port d'Alcúdia
❓ Market held Tue, Sun

Ciutat Romà
🕐 Tue–Fri 10–3.30, Sat–Sun 10–12.45
✋ Inexpensive

Museu Monogràfic de Pollentia
✉ Carrer Sant Jaume 30 ☎ 971 547004
🕐 Tue–Fri 10–3.30, Sat–Sun 10–12.45
✋ Joint entry with Ciutat Romá

2 Badia de Palma

The good, the bad and the ugly sides of Mallorca's tourist development meet along a 25km (15.5-mile) stretch of coast.

The former villages of S'Arenal and Magaluf sit facing each other across Palma Bay. Once upon a time, a fisherman casting his net into the sea at S'Arenal could have gazed around an empty coastline where the only buildings to stand out

would have been Palma's cathedral and castle. Nowadays he would barely be able to distinguish them among a continuous stretch of hotels, a concrete jungle extending all the way to Magaluf. And he wouldn't be there anyway as there are few fish left to catch.

Like it or loathe it, you are bound to spend some time in Palma Bay – even if you are not staying here, you should visit at least once to see some of the best, and the worst, that Mallorca has to offer. Each of the resorts (described separately) has its own character – young or old, British or German, cheap and cheerful or jet-set rich. One moment you can be in Portals Nous, with its chic marina crammed with millionaires' yachts (you have to be seriously rich just to look at the restaurant menus here), the next in seedy Magaluf, all British pubs and wet T-shirt contests.

Occasionally you come across a glimpse of what this coastline must once have been like. Follow the road beyond Magaluf through the pine woods. Suddenly you are among tiny coves where, out of season, you might still find your own private beach. Eventually you reach the headland of Cap de Cala Figuera where you can look back at sweeping views of the entire bay. Cliffs plunge into the clear blue sea, with not a hotel in sight. Come up here at midnight for utter peace and solitude; but listen carefully and you might just be able to hear the disco beat of Magaluf pounding away beneath you.

➕ 137 C5 🍴 Bars and restaurants in all the resorts (€)
🚌 From Palma to all the resorts 🚢 Boat tours of Palma Bay in summer from Palma, S'Arenal, Palma Nova and Magaluf

3 Cap de Formentor

This wild peninsula on Mallorca's northeast tip has stunning views, sandy beaches and the island's original luxury hotel.

The 20km (12.5-mile) drive from Port de Pollença to Mallorca's most northerly point has scenery as dramatic as anyone could wish for. Cliffs 400m (1,310ft) tall jut into the sea, their weird rock formations attracting nesting seabirds, while pine trees seem to grow out of the rocks. The drive is also famously scary – a local legend has it that the parish priest and the local bus driver arrived at the Pearly Gates, and only the driver was admitted to heaven. The reason? He had led far more people to pray.

Six kilometres (4 miles) from Port de Pollença you reach the Mirador des Colomer – scramble up the steps for views over a rocky islet. A path opposite the steps leads to an old watchtower from which you can see the whole of the peninsula as well as the bays of Pollença and Alcúdia. The road continues through pine woods and past more *miradors* (each one helpfully indicated with a picture of an old-fashioned camera) before tunnelling through En Fumat mountain, where you look down over Mallorca's most inaccessible beach. Eventually you reach a lighthouse with the inevitable bar and shop and more stunning views, all the way to Menorca on a good day.

On the way back, stop at Formentor beach and the Hotel Formentor, which opened in 1929 and has been pampering the rich and famous ever since. The fine sandy beach used to be reserved for the hotel's guests, but democracy has opened it to the masses.

➕ 135 A5 🍴 Café with snacks at Cap de Formentor (€); restaurant (€€€) in Hotel Formentor 🚌 From Palma and Port de Pollença in summer 🚢 From Port de Pollença to Formentor beach and Cap de Formentor in summer ❓ The best time to see birds and flowers is spring

4 Castell d'Alaró

A popular walk to a ruined castle and hilltop chapel offering spectacular views all the way to the sea.

A castle has stood on this site since Moorish times; it was so impregnable that the Arab commander was able to hold out for two years after the Christian conquest. Later, in 1285, two heroes of Mallorcan independence, Cabrit and Brassa, defended the castle against Alfonsó III of Aragón and were burned alive on a spit when he finally took it by storm. Their punishment was a consequence of their impudent defiance of the king. They pretended to confuse Alfonso's name with that of a local fish – *anfós*, shouting: 'We like our *anfós* grilled.' The present ruins date from the 15th century and seem almost to grow out of the rock, dominating the landscape for miles around.

The climb up here is one of Mallorca's most popular walks, especially on Sundays. From the town of Alaró it is a stiff climb of about two hours, following the signs from the PM210 to Orient; you can also leave from Orient (➤ 80), following a small path opposite L'Hermitage hotel, again taking around two hours in total. The paths converge above Es Verger restaurant (you can even bring a car this far if you don't mind the potholes and the hairpin bends), where you can fill up with roast lamb to fortify you for the final steep climb.

At last you reach the castle, 800m (2,625ft) above sea level; look back at

the view, stretching across the entire plain to Palma and out to sea. A few minutes further brings you to the summit, with a small chapel and sanctuary, and (bliss!) a restaurant and bar. If you are inspired by the views, you can stay the night here in one of the simple rooms and experience the true tranquillity of the place.

➕ 133 D6 ☎ Sanctuary: 971 182112 ⓐ Open access
🍴 Es Verger (€€) on the way up; simple restaurant (€€) at the sanctuary 🚌 From Palma to Alaró

5 Castell de Bellver

A well-preserved 14th-century royal fortress with fragrant pine woods, an interesting museum and superb views over Palma Bay.

Looking up at this castle, so perfectly maintained, it is hard to believe that it has been standing for almost 700 years. Begun by Jaume II in 1300 and built by Pere Salvà, the architect of the Almudaina Palace, it is unique among Spanish castles in being entirely round. Three large towers surround a central courtyard, connected by an arch to a free-standing keep. The courtyard is on two levels, the ground floor with semicircular arches and a flat roof, the upper level with Gothic arches and rib vaulting. For the full effect, walk around the moat then climb onto the roof and look down into the courtyard to compare the contrasting styles. While

you are there, look out over the city and the bay for one of the best views in Palma (*bellver* means 'lovely view' in Catalan).

For many centuries the castle was used as a prison; Jaume III's widow and sons were imprisoned here for most of their lives. These days it contains Palma's museum of municipal history which traces the development of the city through its artefacts, with pottery from Talaiotic, Roman, Arab and Spanish periods. You can get there by car or taxi, or take a bus to Plaça Gomila and climb up through the pine woods above Carrer de Bellver, passing a chapel on the way.

✠ 136 B4 ✉ Carrer Camilo José Cela s/n, Parc Bellver ☎ 971 730657
🕓 Apr–Sep Mon–Sat 8–8.30, Sun 10–7; Oct–Mar Mon–Sat 8–7.15, Sun 10–5
✋ Inexpensive. Free entrance on Sun, when museum closed 🚍 3 or 6 to Plaça Gomila, or city sightseeing bus direct to the castle ❓ Evening concerts Jul, Aug

6 Coves d'Artà

A fascinating network of underground caverns, whose weird stalactites and stalagmites conjure up mysterious images of Heaven and Hell.

If you only have time to visit one set of caves on the east coast, this is the one to see. Now that they are a sanitised tourist attraction, it is hard to imagine how French geologist Édouard Martel felt when he first stepped into these caves, dark, mysterious and terrifying, in 1876. In fact they had

been known about for centuries – Jaume I found 2,000 Arabs hiding here with their cattle during the Christian conquest, and they were later used by hermits, pirates and smugglers – but it was Martel who first studied and chronicled these grottoes, 46m (150ft) above the sea at Cap Vermell, at the instigation of Archduke Ludwig Salvator. Another early visitor was Jules Verne; the caves are said to have inspired his *Journey to the Centre of the Earth*.

The guided tour comes with special effects and the various chambers are given Dantesque names – Hell, Purgatory, Paradise. The descent into Hell is swiftly followed by a *son et lumière* display. Stalactites point down from the mouldy roof like daggers, somehow defying gravity. One of the chambers is as large as the nave of Palma Cathedral, and the Queen of Pillars, a stalagmite 22m (72ft) tall, could almost be a Gothic column. It is growing upwards at the rate of 2cm (0.7in) every 100 years; in another 5,000 years or so it will be joined to the ceiling.

You emerge from the caves to a view of the sea, framed by the cavern entrance. Disabled visitors and others with limited mobility will find the staircases in here particularly difficult. All visitors should be sensibly shod, as the floor can be slippery.

✚ 135 E7 ☎ 971 841293 ◷ Jul–Sep daily 10–7; Oct–Jun daily 10–5 👋 Expensive 🍴 Bars at Platja de Canyamel near by (€) 🚌 From Artà and Cala Rajada in summer

7 Deià

An idyllic village of green-shuttered, ochre-coloured houses has become a millionaires' hideaway in the shadow of the Teix mountain.

Deià could have been just another pretty Mallorcan village had Robert Graves not decided to make it his home. The English poet and novelist first moved here in 1932 with his mistress Laura Riding and returned in 1946 with his second wife. Muses followed, friends came to stay, and before long Deià had established a reputation as a foreign artists' colony. Now it is on every tourist itinerary as the prime example of 'the other Mallorca' and this small village contains two luxury hotels. Rich foreign residents, like the actor Michael Douglas, are apt to bemoan the arrival of tour buses; the few locals who remain are philosophical about outsiders.

Graves was hardly the first to discover Deià. An 1878 guidebook noted its 'collection of strange and eccentric

foreigners' and it has stayed that way ever since. Climb the Carrer es Puig, Deià's only real street, passing ceramic Stations of the Cross, to reach the parish church and the small cemetery where Graves is buried. His tombstone, like many others, is inscribed in simple handwriting set into the drying concrete –

Robert Graves, Poeta, 1895–1985.
Graves' house, Ca n'Alluny, has been
acquired by the government and
turned into a museum.

From Deià you can scramble down
to Cala de Deià, a small shingle beach
set in an attractive cove, where local
artists still continue the Graves
tradition of naked swimming and long
parties at weekends.

🞢 133 D5 🍴 Wide choice of restaurants and bars (€–€€€)
🚌 From Palma, Valldemossa and Port de Sóller
❓ Classical music festival Aug–Sep

8 Lluc

Mallorca's most sacred site – a former monastery in a spectacular setting in the Serra de Tramuntana.

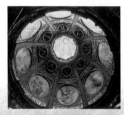

Lluc has been a centre of pilgrimage since the 13th century when an Arab shepherd boy discovered a dark wooden statue of the Virgin. The image was put in the local church but three times it returned miraculously to its cave, whereupon the villagers recognized a message from God and built a chapel to house it.

La Moreneta ('the Little Dark One') is now encrusted with precious stones, and sits in a chapel decorated with the arms of every Mallorcan town. Pilgrims and tourists queue to pay homage, especially on Sundays and at 11am before the daily concerts by Els Blauets choir. The choir, named after their blue cassocks, was established in 1531, comprising 40 boys, 'natives of Mallorca, of pure blood, sound in grammar and song'. The service is marred by the whirring and flashing of cameras, and if it's meditation you seek, come back instead for the evening Mass.

The monastery complex includes Els Porxets, the former pilgrims' quarters with stabling beneath the rooms, and the Way of the Rosary, with touches by Antoni Gaudí. From the hilltop cross you look down over a farmland valley and up into the pine-covered mountains. You can stay at Lluc but it is more like a hotel than a hermitage – the 100 'cells' have *en suite* bathrooms and there are several restaurants and bars. There is also a museum – among the displays of ceramics, chalices and coins is a collection of paintings by the 20th-century Mallorcan artist Josep Coll Bardolet, with scenes from Deià, Valldemossa and Fornalutx.

🕂 133 C7 ☎ 971 871525 🕓 Museum: daily 10–1.30, 2.30–5.15. Monastery: daily 9–8.30 💰 Monastery: free; museum: inexpensive 🍴 Sa Fonda (€€) in the former monks' refectory 🚌 Two buses daily from Palma and Inca ❓ Choir concert daily at 11.15 during Mass; second service at dusk open to those staying; annual night-time pilgrimage from Palma to Lluc on foot (48km/30 miles), usually held in first week of Aug

9 La Seu (Palma Cathedral)

The glory of Palma – a magnificent Gothic cathedral whose sandstone walls and flying buttresses seem to rise out of the sea.

Anything you see inside Palma cathedral will come as a disappointment once you have stood on the seafront and gazed up at its golden sandstone exterior, climbing above the old city walls. La Seu stands out from its surroundings, a demonstration of the might of Mallorca's Christian conquerors to all who arrived by sea.

Tradition has it that a storm arose as Jaume I was sailing towards Mallorca. He vowed that if he landed safely he would build a great church in honour of the Virgin. On New Year's Day 1230, a day after the fall of Palma, the foundation stone was symbolically laid on the site of the city's main mosque. Work continued for 400 years – and had to resume in 1851 when an earthquake destroyed the west front. More touches were added in the 20th century by the Catalan architect Antoni Gaudí.

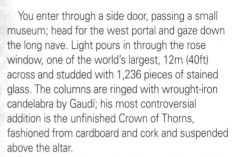

You enter through a side door, passing a small museum; head for the west portal and gaze down the long nave. Light pours in through the rose window, one of the world's largest, 12m (40ft) across and studded with 1,236 pieces of stained glass. The columns are ringed with wrought-iron candelabra by Gaudí; his most controversial addition is the unfinished Crown of Thorns, fashioned from cardboard and cork and suspended above the altar.

Be sure to walk around to the south front, facing the sea, to look at the Portal del Mirador, a 15th-century door by Guillem Sagrera featuring scenes from the Last Supper.

✚ 141 E5 ✉ Plaça d'Almoina ☎ 971 723130 ◷ Jun–Sep Mon–Fri 10–6.15, Sat 10–2.15; Apr–May, Oct Mon–Fri 10–5.15, Sat 10–2.15; Nov–Mar Mon–Fri 10–3.15, Sat 10–2.15 👜 Moderate (free for services) ❓ High Mass Sun 10.30

10 Valldemossa

This small town in the mountains is where Mallorcan tourism began one cold, damp winter in 1838.

Try as it might Valldemossa cannot escape its connection with Frédéric Chopin and his lover George Sand. They arrived in 1838, having rented a former monk's cell, planning to carry on their affair away from the gossip of Paris and hoping that the

climate would benefit Chopin's health (he had TB). Nothing worked out as planned. The weather was wet, the couple were shunned by the locals, Chopin's piano failed to arrive and the relationship never recovered. Sand took out her anger on Valldemossa in a spiteful book, *Winter in Majorca*, labelling the locals as thieves and savages.

The **Reial Cartoixa** (Royal Carthusian Monastery) is the focus of any visit – white-arched corridors lead to 'cells' containing museums on various themes. Visit the old pharmacy, then look into the library, where the monks would meet for half an hour a week, their only human contact. There is a fine modern art museum, with works by Picasso, Miró and Juli Ramis.

Most people come for the Chopin experience, but there is more to Valldemossa than that. It is also the birthplace of Catalina Thomás, Mallorca's patron saint. Born in 1531, she became a nun in Palma and was renowned for her humility. Her birthplace at Carrer Rectoría 5 has been turned into a shrine.

The newest attraction in Valldemossa is Michael Douglas' Costa Nord (➤ 77).

✚ 132 D4 🍴 Restaurants and bars (€€) 🚌 From Palma, Deià and Port de Sóller ❓ Regular Chopin piano concerts in Palau del Rei Sanç (entered on same ticket as monastery); La Beata procession in honour of Santa Catalina Thomás, 27–28 Jul; Chopin Festival in Aug; market held Sun

Reial Cartoixa

☎ 971 612106 🕐 Mar–Oct Mon–Sat 9.30–6, Sun 10–1; Nov–Feb, Mon–Sat 9.30–4.30 💰 Expensive

Exploring

Each region of Mallorca has its own particular appeal – Palma for its thriving arts scene and lively café society, the northeast for history, the east coast for beaches and caves, the north and west for spectacular mountains and picture-postcard villages. And you haven't seen Mallorca until you have driven across *es pla*, the fertile plain at the centre of the island, with its almond groves, windmills and old market towns.

Try to do a bit of everything – one monastery, one mountain walk, one quiet cove – but don't try to do too much. The twisting mountain roads get very crowded in summer and journeys take longer than you think. Take your time and avoid the worst of the heat by doing what the Mallorcans do, break for a siesta. It is generally far more rewarding to spend a day pottering around one small area than to hare from one town to another ticking off the sights.

Palma

**Known to the Arabs as Medina Mayurqa
and to Mallorcans simply as *Ciutat*
(City), Palma is in fact named after the
Roman city of Palmaria. Here you can almost literally
uncover the different layers of Mallorcan history. The
Roman city still exists, a metre or two beneath the
ground; inhabitants of houses near the cathedral are
still discovering Roman remains. The cathedral was
built on the site of a mosque, once a Roman temple;
the royal palace replaced an Arab *alcázar*.**

The city you see today, however, is a relatively recent creation.
The tree-lined promenades of La Rambla and Passeig des Born,
home to florists and newspaper sellers, were built in the 19th
century on a dried-up river bed. The walls that once surrounded the
city were pulled down to create the ring road Las Avingudas, and
Passeig Marítim, the waterfront highway and promenade,
was only reclaimed from the sea in the 1950s.

Most of the main sights are located within the area bounded
by the old walls, especially to the north and east of the cathedral.
Wander along any alley in the ancient Arab quarter, peering
through wrought-iron gates and heavy wooden doors, and you will
be rewarded with glimpses of one magnificent patio after another,
with their stone staircases, galleries and arcades.

But you have not truly seen
Palma until you have surveyed
it from the waterfront, with the
cathedral and Almudaina palace
rising proudly above the
defensive walls of the old city,
their golden sandstone lit up by
the afternoon sun.

✚ 137 B5

ℹ Tourist information ➤ 16

45

BANYS ÀRABS

These 10th-century baths are virtually all that remain of the Arab city of Medina Mayurqa. They were probably part of a nobleman's house and are similar to those found in other Islamic cities. The *tepidarium* has a dome in the shape of a half-orange, with 25 round shafts for sunlight, supported by a dozen columns. Notice how each of the columns is different – they were probably salvaged from the ruins of various Roman buildings, an early example of recycling. *Hammams* were meeting places as well as wash-houses, and the courtyard with its cactus, palm and orange trees would have made a pleasant place to cool off after a hot bath.

✚ 141 F6 ✉ Carrer Can Serra 7 ☎ 971 721549 🕐 Apr–Nov daily 9–7; Dec–Mar daily 9–6 🍴 Inexpensive 🍴 Bar Sa Murada nearby (€)

BASÍLICA DE SANT FRANCESC

The façade of this 13th-century church (remodelled after it was struck by lightning in the 17th century) is typically Mallorcan – a massive, forbidding sandstone wall with a delicately carved portal and a rose window at the centre. You enter through peaceful Gothic cloisters with orange and lemon trees and a well at the centre. Inside the church is the tomb of Ramón Llull (1235–1316), the Catalan mystic who became a hermit following a failed seduction attempt and was later stoned to death attempting to convert Muslims in Tunisia. His statue can be seen on the Palma seafront; outside the basilica is a statue of another famous Mallorcan missionary, Fray Junípero Serra, who once lived in the monastery here. The streets behind the church, once home to jewellers and Jewish traders, are now rundown and seedy and best avoided after dark.

✚ 141 D6 ✉ Plaça Sant Francesc ☎ 971 712695 🕐 Mon–Sat 9.30–12.30, 3.30–6, Sun 9.30–12.30
💷 Inexpensive

CASTELL DE BELLVER

See pages 30–31.

ES BALUARD

Opened in 2004 and set inside the restored 16th-century bastion of Sant Pere, this museum dramatically combines military architecture with modern art. The displays vary but will probably include work by Picasso, Joan Miró and Miquel Barceló. A walk around the walls offers spectacular views over the bay, and there are more good views from the sculpture terrace.

🕂 140 D2 ✉ Plaça Porta de Santa Catalina ☎ 971 908200 🕐 Mid-Jun to Sep Tue–Sun 10am–11pm; Oct to mid-Jun Tue–Sun 10–8 ✋ Moderate

FUNDACIÓ LA CAIXA

The Gran Hotel was Palma's first luxury hotel when it opened in 1903. Designed by Lluís Domènech i Montaner, it began the craze for *modernista* (art nouveau) architecture in the city. Restored by the Fundació la Caixa and reopened in 1993, it is now an art gallery with changing exhibitions and paintings by Hermen Anglada-Camarasa, founder of the 'Pollença school'. On the ground floor is a bookshop and a trendy café-bar.

🕂 141 C5 ✉ Plaça Weyler 3 ☎ 971 178500 🕐 Tue–Sat 10–9, Sun 10–2 ✋ Free 🍴 Café and restaurant (€€)

FUNDACIÓ PILAR I JOAN MIRÓ

The painter and sculptor Joan Miró spent most of his life in Barcelona, but both his wife and mother were Mallorcan and he always longed to return to the scene of his childhood holidays to draw inspiration from what he called 'the light of Mallorca'. In 1956, aged 63, he bought a house and studio in Cala Major. He lived here until he died in 1983 after which it was enlarged to hold a permanent exhibition of his works.

The collection includes more than 100 paintings, 25 sculptures and 3,000 studio pieces but only a small amount is displayed at any time. The paintings are almost childish, all vivid splashes of bright primary colours, influenced by his love of peasant traditions and his fascination with *siurells* (clay whistles). Anyone tempted to remark that their child could do better should take a look at the heavily realistic work that Miró was producing aged eight – the fantasy came later. Works on display include the draft for UNESCO's *Mural del Sol* in Paris.

Glance into Miró's studio, left untouched since his death, with work in progress, open tins of paint and black stains all over the floor.

✚ 137 B4 ✉ Carrer Joan de Saridakis 29, Cala Major ☎ 971 701420
🕐 15 May–15 Sep Tue–Sat 10–7, Sun 10–3; 16 Sep–14 May Tue–Sat 10–6, Sun 10–3 🎫 Moderate 🍽 Café (€) 🚌 6 from Palma

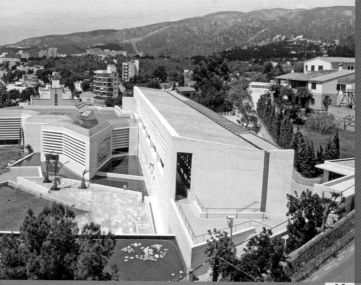

a walk around Palma

Start on Plaça d'Espanya by the statue of Jaume I the Conqueror on horseback. With the station behind you, bear left across the square towards Mercat Olivar (➤ 52–53).

Leave via Plaça Olivar and turn left into Carrer Sant Miquel.

Soon you reach Plaça Major with its outdoor cafés and street entertainers.

Continue across the square; fork right into Carrer Jaume II.

At the end of this pedestrian shopping street, don't fail to look up at the Moorish-style *modernista* façade of Can Corbella before turning left into Plaça Cort. Beyond a gnarled olive tree you see the town hall.

Take the short street to the left of the town hall to reach Plaça Santa Eulàlia; cross this square diagonally and take Carrer Morey.

This brings you into the heart of the old city. Take your time here admiring the courtyards; don't miss Casa Oleza at No 9.

Continue straight on to Carrer Miramar and turn right onto the city walls.

The cathedral (➤ 38–39) is above you; to visit it and the palace, climb the steps to a large wooden cross.

Back on the walls, continue until you drop to the S'Hort del Rei gardens (➤ 54). Cross Plaça Reina and walk up the Born (➤ 57), turning right by Bar Bosch into Carrer Unió.

Look out for the old Gran Hotel (➤ 48) on your left and the bakery opposite, two good examples of *modernista* style. Beyond the theatre, the road bends left and becomes La Rambla; stroll up this promenade among the flower stalls.

At the top of La Rambla, turn right into Carrer Oms and follow it back to Plaça d'Espanya.

Distance 3.5km (2 miles)
Time 2 hours; with coffee, browsing and visits – probably half a day

Start/end point Plaça d'Espanya ✛ 141 A7
🚌 Most city buses terminate here; island buses terminate at the nearby bus station on Carrer Eusebi Estada 🚆 Trains from Inca and Sóller also terminate here
Lunch Fundació la Caixa (€) ✉ Plaça Weyler 3
☎ 971 728077

LA LLOTJA

With twin turrets and an angel over the door, this 15th-century seafront building looks half-castle, half-church. In fact it is neither. It was designed by Guillem Sagrera (the architect of the cathedral's Portal del Mirador) as the city's exchange. Stand among the spiralling pillars, gaze up at the rib vaulting, and try to imagine the merchants of 500 years ago haggling over silk, spices and silver. Nowadays La Llotja is a cultural centre, hosting temporary exhibitions.

🚩 140 E3 ☎ 971 711705 ✉ Plaça Llotja ⏰ Exhibitions only: Tue–Sat 11–2, 5–7, Sun 11–2 🎫 Free 🍴 Wide choice of restaurants and bars nearby (€–€€)

MERCAT OLIVAR

When you're tired of museums and churches and want to meet the people of Palma instead, head for this large covered market near Plaça d'Espanya. After a recent renovation, there is now a supermarket on the first floor and the ground-floor stalls have been spruced up but the market has lost none of its atmosphere.

Huge piles of oranges and tomatoes, buckets full of olives, meat and cheese counters and fresh fish stalls in a separate annex all add up to a visual feast. There are also several traditional *tapas* bars, where the market workers can still be seen drinking brandy with their breakfast coffee.

➕ 141 B7 ✉ Plaça Olivar ☎ 971 720315 ⏱ Mon–Sat 8–2 ✋ Free
🍽 Several *tapas* bars (€) upstairs

MUSEU D'ART ESPANYOL CONTEMPORANI

The private collection of Mallorcan banker Joan March (1880–1962) has been expanded into this small museum of 20th-century Spanish art close to Plaça Major. Among the artists represented are Picasso, Joan Miró and Salvador Dalí, Catalan abstract artist Antoni Tàpies and Basque sculptor Eduardo Chillida. A room is dedicated to Miquel Barceló, the avant-garde painter born in Mallorca in 1957.

➕ 141 C6 ✉ Carrer Sant Miquel 11 ☎ 971 713515 ⏱ Mon–Fri 10–6.30, Sat 10.30–2 ✋ Free

MUSEU DE MALLORCA

Mallorca's most important museum is housed in a
17th-century palace, with collections spanning more
than 3,000 years of history. Start in the basement prehistory
section, which includes pottery, metal and stone artefacts from
the Talaiotic cultures, as well as bronze figures of naked warriors
brought back from the Punic wars. Other rooms are devoted to
Islamic archaeology, Gothic art (with a particularly fine collection of
painted altarpieces), Modernism and 20th-century art.

➕ 141 E6 ✉ Carrer Portella 5 ☎ 971 717540 🕐 Tue–Sat 10–7, Sun 10–2
🎟 Inexpensive 🍴 Bar Sa Murada (€) at foot of Carrer Portella

PALAU DE L'ALMUDAINA

A royal palace has stood on this site
since the Muslim *walis* (governors)
built their *alcázar* soon after the
Arab conquest. It was converted
into Gothic style, but elements of
Islamic architecture remain – like
the Moorish arches seen from the
seafront, lit up at night like a row of lanterns. The courtyard,
flanked by palm trees, is at its best in late afternoon when the
sun falls on the cathedral towers overhead. Just off the courtyard
is the royal chapel, Capella de Santa Ana.

The S'Hort del Rei gardens beneath the palace make a pleasant
place to sit beneath the fountains watching the world go by. Look
out for the Arc de la Drassana, once the gateway to the royal
docks; near here is a statue of a *hondero* or Balearic slinger. The
gardens were rebuilt in the 1960s, forcing the demolition of
several houses; their best-known landmark is Joan Miró's *Egg*
sculpture, which few can resist sticking their heads through.

➕ 140 E4 ✉ Carrer Palau Reial ☎ 971 214134 🕐 Palace: Apr–Sep
Mon–Fri 10–6.30, Sat 10–2; Oct–Mar Mon–Fri 10–2, 4–6, Sat 10–2. Gardens:
open access 🎟 Palace: moderate; gardens: free

PALAU MARCH

This quirky museum reflects the eclectic tastes of the banker Joan March and his son Bartolomé. Most striking is the sculpture terrace, in an open courtyard surrounded by an attractive loggia in the shadow of the cathedral. Among the artists represented are Rodin, Henry Moore, Barbara Hepworth and contemporary Spanish sculptors. Highlights include miniature Neapolitan crib figures, 16th-century Mallorcan maps, and the original 1940s murals for the Music Room by Josep Maria Sert, with acrobats and carnival scenes.

✚ 140 E4 ✉ Carrer Palau Reial 18 ☎ 971 711122 ⏰ Apr–Oct Mon–Fri 10–6.30; Nov–Mar Mon–Fri 10–5, Sat 10–2 ✋ Moderate 🍴 Cappuccino Palau March (€)

PASSEIG DES BORN

For more than a century this short, tree-lined promenade has been at the heart of city life; it has witnessed *festas*, demonstrations and countless generations of families enjoying an evening stroll. During the Franco era it was renamed after the dictator, but everyone still called it 'the Born'. Come here to take the pulse of Palma from a seat at a pavement café – Bar Bosch, near the top of the Born in Plaça Rei Joan Carles I, is the traditional place. Near here is **Ca'n Solleric,** a modern art gallery in a converted mansion that also houses the city's tourist office.

140 D4 Choice of restaurants and cafés nearby (€–€€)

Ca'n Solleric

Passeig des Born 27 971 722092 Tue–Sat 10–2, 5–9, Sun 10–1.30 Free

POBLE ESPANYOL (SPANISH VILLAGE)

Spain gets the theme-park treatment at this 'village' in the outskirts of Palma, where reproductions of famous buildings from Córdoba, Toledo and Madrid are gathered together with typical houses from the Spanish regions. You can eat Spanish food in the Plaza Mayor (Spanish spellings here) or sit outside a café watching the tourists buy pearls and souvenirs at the village shops. A visit here gives you a whistle-stop tour of Spanish architecture, showing its development through Muslim and then Christian influences. If you have never been to Granada, it's worth coming just for the reproduction of the salon, baths and patio from the Alhambra Palace. Various artists give displays of handicrafts in workshops scattered throughout the 'village'.

✚ 140 E1 (off map) ✉ Carrer Poble Espanyol 39 ☎ 971 737075 ⏱ Daily 9–6; shops closed Sat afternoon and Sun 🍴 Restaurant and cafés (€€) 🚌 5 ♿ Moderate ❓ Craft displays from 10 to one hour before closing time

LA SEU (PALMA CATHEDRAL)

See pages 38–39.

West of Palma

The west side of Mallorca has examples of all the geographical features and characteristics to be found on the rest of the island, including beautiful beaches, busy resorts, a more rugged northern coastline as well as some fine mountain scenery. Some of the earlier built hotels remain along the coastline where tiny fishing villages once were, but new building is far more regulated and sympathetic to the environment and some of the ugliest hotels have been replaced by palm-fringed promenades.

The Bay of Palma is popular still with millionaires and nearby Cala Major is the summer home of King Juan Carlos and Queen Sofía of Spain. The marina at Puerto Portals is filled with the yachts of the rich and famous and celebrities such as racing driver Michael Schumacher and supermodel Claudia Schiffer have holiday homes at chic Camp de Mar.

However, the hinterland has remained unspoiled and you can still find traditional Mallorcan villages, such as Puigpunyent, where time goes at the most gentle of paces and you feel as though you have 'got away from it all'.

ANDRATX

Like many towns around the coast, Andratx was built some way
inland from its port to deter pirate raids. These days the town is
reaping an unexpected benefit – tourists pour into the port,
spending money which the town collects in taxes, except on
market day when Andratx sees little of the visitors and its people
are left to get on with their lives. Surrounded by orange groves
and almond trees, Andratx is a sleepy town which only really gets
animated on Wednesdays when the streets are taken over by
market stalls selling vegetables, cheeses and fish. When you have
finished your shopping, climb to the top of the town to see the
13th-century church of Santa Maria.

✚ 136 B2 🍴 Bars and cafés (€) 🚌 Regular buses from Palma, Peguera and
Port d'Andratx ❓ Market held Wed

BANYALBUFAR

People come to Banyalbufar to see one thing – its terraced
hillsides, sloping down to the sea. Developed by the Moors and

divided by drystone walls, these terraces speak powerfully of man's ingenuity in creating farmland out of inhospitable cliffs. Until recently it was the custom for each generation to add a further tier. In Moorish times the town, whose Arabic name means 'vineyard by the sea', was famed for its Malvasia wine – nowadays the terraces are mostly used to grow vegetables, though a few vines have been planted once again.

Banyalbufar's popularity with foreign artists has led some people to conclude that it will be the next Deià (➤ 34–35). 🚩 132 E3 🍴 Café Bellavista (€) 🚌 Bus from Palma

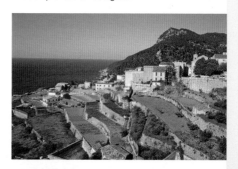

a drive around the West

This drive gives an excellent introduction to the mountain and coastal scenery of western Mallorca.

Start in Andratx, taking the C710 to Estellencs about halfway up the main street.

Immediately the road begins to climb through pine woods and tunnels, with occasional glimpses of the sea. Follow this beautiful twisting coast road to the village of Estellencs, one of the prettiest in Mallorca, with narrow, steep cobbled streets and women doing their washing at the village well. After another 5km (3 miles), stop at the Mirador de Ses Animes and clamber up to the 16th-century watchtower for views right along the northwest coast. Soon after this you reach Banyalbufar (➤ 60–61), with its spectacular terracing.

When the C710 turns off left towards Valldemossa, keep straight on the PM110, signposted to Palma. After 1km (0.5 miles) you see a sign to La Granja on your right.

You could easily spend 2 to 3 hours at this display of Mallorcan traditions (➤ 66).

Leaving La Granja, take the narrow road to Puigpunyent from the car park.

Follow this road for 10km (6 miles), a dramatic journey through olive groves in the shadow of Puig de Galatzó. The road continues through Puigpunyent and on to Galilea (► 65), a mountain village with a couple of *tapas* bars and views out to sea. From here the road twists and turns down to the village of Es Capdellà.

Turn right in the village and follow signs back to Andratx.

Distance 62km (38 miles)
Time 3 hours plus lunch and time at La Granja
Start/end point Andratx ✚ 136 B2
Lunch La Granja (€) ☎ 971 610032

420 dC
DESTRUCCION
DE
POLLENTIA
POR LOS
VANDALOS

1248
CALVIA QUEDA
CONSTITUIDA EN
PARROQUIA

1233
NACE RAMON LLULL

1208
NACE EL REY JAIME I
EN MONTPELLER

904
LOS
ARABES
CONQUISTAN
MALLORCA

123 aC
CONQUISTA
DE MALLORCA
POR LOS
ROMANOS

HABITANTES
DE CALVIA
A TRAVES DE
LOS TIEMPOS

1248	CALVIA QUEDA CONSTITUIDA EN PARROQUIA POR BULA DEL PAPA INOCENCIO IV
1285	80 HABITANTES
1511	128 "
1543	256 "
1600	431 "
1700	856 "
1800	1656 "
1900	2567 "
1930	2617 "
1940	5463 "
1950	2327 "
1960	3005 "
1970	4990 "
1980	11560 "

400 aC
HONDEROS
BALEARES

ORICO
FICO
NO DE
A

COSTA DE
BENDNAT

CALVIÀ

Until recently an unassuming country town, Calvià hit the jackpot when tourists discovered the nearby beaches and it is now said to be the richest municipality in Spain. There are a few ostentatious signs of wealth, like the sparkling new town hall and sports stadium, but mostly life continues as before, with ochre-coloured houses, a handful of shops and bars, and chickens scrambling between the olive trees. The town is dominated by the church of Sant Joan Baptista, built in the late 19th century around the 13th-century original; near here, by a fountain, a ceramic mural tells the story of Calvià's history. Founded in 1249 with 80 inhabitants, the town had a population of 3,000 in 1960 and 11,560 in 1980 – all because of tourism. Stand on the terrace looking out over almond and carob trees and it is hard to believe you are just a few kilometres from the teeming resorts of 'Maganova'.

✚ 136 B3 🍴 Restaurants and bars (€€) 🚌 From Palma ❓ Market on Mon

GALILEA

This pretty village, 460m (1,510ft) above sea level, in the shadow of the great peak of Puig de Galatzó, gets crowded out by day trippers who come to sample the views from the church terrace. On a good day you can see far out to sea, while eating *tapas* outside the church and listening to the echo of sheep-bells on the hillsides. The nearby village of Puigpunyent

is also justifiably popular and is surrounded by orange groves – as well as being the base for visiting La Reserva (➤ 72).

✚ 136 A3 🍴 Two bars (€)

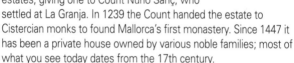

LA GRANJA

This country house, just south of Banyalbufar, is on a site known since Roman times for its natural spring. When Jaume I conquered Mallorca he divided the island into four feudal estates, giving one to Count Nuno Sanç, who settled at La Granja. In 1239 the Count handed the estate to Cistercian monks to found Mallorca's first monastery. Since 1447 it has been a private house owned by various noble families; most of what you see today dates from the 17th century.

Highlights of the tour include an aristocratic drawing-room with its own theatre, the family chapel and a dungeon with a torture chamber – but the real reason for visiting is to learn about rural Mallorcan traditions. Workshops, cellars and kitchens contain displays of everyday objects. On Wednesday and Friday afternoons, women in traditional costume give demonstrations of lacemaking, embroidery and spinning, donkeys turn threshing-wheels and there are tastings of cheese, wine, sausages, doughnuts and fig cake. There are also displays of bagpipe music and folk dancing, which are entertaining if not terribly authentic.

Escape from the tour groups by walking in the grounds, which contain botanical gardens, waterfalls and a thousand-year-old yew – there is a 1.2km (0.7-mile) signed walk. La Granja is still a working farm and you may see pigs, turkeys, chickens and goats, as well as displays of agricultural implements and tools.

The restaurant serves good Mallorcan staples like *pa amb oli* and *sopes mallorquines*.

www.lagranja.net
✚ 132 E4 ✉ Carrer Esporles Puigpunyent, km2 Esporles ☎ 971 610032 🕐 Apr–Sep daily 10–7; Oct–Mar daily 10–6 💷 Expensive
🍴 Restaurant (€) 🚌 From Palma
❓ Folk fiesta, Wed, Fri 3.30–5

MAGALUF

More than anywhere else in Mallorca, Magaluf has been blighted by the curse of mass tourism. During the 1980s it became a byword for all that was wrong with Mallorca; foreign TV crews would flock here to film drinking competitions, wet T-shirt contests and teenagers throwing up on the beach. However, in the 1990s Magaluf tried hard to change its image. High-rise hotels have been destroyed, a

new seafront promenade has been built, and the council has introduced activities from guided walks to *tai chi* on the beach. But still the lager louts come...and if you want cheap sun, sea, sand and *sangría*, there's no better place.

➕ 136 C3 🍴 Bars and restaurants (€) 🚌 Regular buses from Palma

PALMA NOVA

There are people who can remember when this was just a village; then along came the tourist boom, and 'new Palma' became the favoured resort of the British. More restrained than Magaluf, less exclusive than Portals Nous, Palma Nova occupies a prime position on the western side of the bay of Palma. It makes a good base for a family holiday, with nearby attractions including Aqualand Magaluf and Marineland – as long as you don't mind sharing your family holiday with a thousand others.

➕ 136 C3 🍴 Wide choice of restaurants (€–€€)
🚌 Regular buses from Palma

PEGUERA

This beach resort, popular with German tour operators, was the first in Mallorca to have its own artificial beach. Once on the main road from Palma to Andratx, it has become much more peaceful since the construction of a bypass and the opening of a seafront promenade. Just outside Peguera is Cala Fornells, a chic resort of terracotta houses set around a pretty cove. Nearby Camp de Mar is a fast-growing resort where racing driver Michael Schumacher and model Claudia Schiffer both have homes.

➕ 136 B2 🍴 Wide choice of restaurants (€–€€)
🚌 From Palma

PORT D'ANDRATX

Dress up to come here, or you will feel seriously out of place. Port d'Andratx is one of Mallorca's classiest resorts, popular with the yachting fraternity and with film stars whose Italian-style villas can be seen climbing up the hillsides. But don't let that put you off; come here all the same. The harbour is one of the prettiest in Mallorca and a table at one of the waterside bars is really the perfect place to watch the sunset.

✚ 136 B2 🍴 Wide choice of restaurants (€€–€€€) 🚌 From Andratx

PORTALS NOUS

This is one of the more exclusive resorts in the bay of Palma – not many high-rise hotels here, just rows of private villas and apartments dominating the shoreline. Puerto Portals marina, opened in 1987, is the summer home of the jet set. King Juan Carlos has been known to moor here while staying at his summer palace, Marivent, in nearby Cala Major, and the younger royals can be seen frequenting the waterfront restaurants and bars. Don't even think about looking in the smart boutiques unless you have a high credit card limit.

✚ 136 B4 🍴 Wide choice of bars and restaurants (€€–€€€) 🚌 From Palma

PORTALS VELLS

A bumpy track from Magaluf leads through pine woods to this beautiful cove at the southwest tip of Palma Bay. In summer it gets crowded, but out of season you could have your own private beach, with golden sand, rocky cliffs and shimmering turquoise water. In fact there are two beaches; the smaller one, El Mago, is Mallorca's official nudist beach. From the main beach, hike along the cliffs to the Cove de la Mare de Déu, a rock chapel built by fishermen to give thanks for a safe landing. Back on the road, another 2km (1.2 miles) brings you to the headland of Cap de Cala Figuera, with sweeping views of the entire bay of Palma.

🚲 136 C3 🍴 Beach bar and restaurant (€€) 🚌 From Palma Oct–May Mon–Fri (☎ 971 717190)

LA RESERVA

On the slopes of Puig de Galatzó near the village of Puigpunyent, this nature reserve describes itself as 'Mallorca's paradise'. A 3km

(2-mile) trail of waymarked paths leads you through Mallorca's mountain scenery in less than two hours, past waterfalls and springs, olive trees and charcoal stoves. A series of boards provides information on wildlife and mountain industries. Well laid out and interesting, the reserve gives you a feeling for the area. It will seem a bit sterile if you have been out in the mountains on your own, but it may help you make sense of what you have already seen.

✚ 136 A3 ☎ 971 616622 ⚙ Apr–Oct daily 10–7; Nov–Mar daily 10–6 ✋ Expensive 🍴 Café (€)

SA DRAGONERA

This uninhabited island, about 1km (0.5 miles) off Mallorca's western tip, was the focus for a turning point in Mallorcan history in 1977, when it was occupied by environmentalists protesting against a planned tourist development. The campaigners won, the island became a nature reserve instead, the seabirds survived, and for the first time the authorities realized that mass tourism had reached its limit.

Six kilometres (4 miles) long and crowned by an ancient watchtower, Sa Dragonera takes its name from its shape, said to resemble a dragon. You can visit in summer by boat from Sant Elm; in winter you have to make do with views of the dragon from the beach at Sant Elm or from the climb to Sa Trapa (▶ opposite).

✚ 136 B1 🚢 From Sant Elm (☎ 639 617545)

SANT ELM

The main reason for visiting Sant Elm, a laid-back resort with a fine sandy beach, is for the views of Sa Dragonera (➤ opposite). You can take a boat to the island from the jetty at the end of the main street, or sit outside the fish restaurants on the same jetty.

A challenging walk from Sant Elm leads to the abandoned

Trappist monastery of Sa Trapa. Set out on Avinguda de la Trapa and climb through coastal *maquis* and pine, with fine views of Sa Dragonera. The round trip takes about 3 hours; a longer route is signposted beside the cemetery on the Sant Elm to Andratx road. Near here is the village of S'Arracó, built by Spanish settlers returning from the American colonies.

➕ 136 B1 🍴 Choice of restaurants (€€) 🚌 From Andratx or Peguera
⛴ From Port d'Andratx and Peguera in summer

SANTA PONÇA

Santa Ponça may look like just another beach resort but it has a permanent place in Mallorcan history. It was here that Jaume I landed in 1229 to begin his conquest of Mallorca, a conquest he described as 'the best thing man has done for a hundred years past'. A relief on a large cross above the marina, erected in 1929, records the event.

🕇 136 C3 🍴 Bars and restaurants (€–€€) 🚌 From Palma ❓ Rei en Jaume regatta in Jul

SES ILLETES

This genteel resort, with its white villas and old-fashioned hotels, is for many people the most attractive in the whole Badia de Palma. Two small beaches look out over a pair of *illetes* (islets), the larger one crowned by an old watchtower. Its proximity to Palma means that you will never be alone here; in summer the buses from Palma to Ses Illetes are packed out at weekends. But if you want a base near the capital, combining a city break with a beach holiday, this could be just the place.

🕇 136 B4 🍴 Cafés and restaurants (€€) 🚌 From Palma

Tramuntana

Threading along the northwest coast of the island from Sa Dragonera to Cape Formentor is the Tramuntana mountain range. Many rock-climbers and walkers head to this wild, dramatic landscape that is visible from all over Mallorca. The highest peaks top 1,000m (3,280ft), with Puig Major rising to 1,445m (4,740ft) and unmistakable because of the two white globes of the communications complex that sits atop the peak.

Tourism is the main source of income in this part of the island and nestled in the mountains are Lluc and Deià, along with luxurious hotels clustered throughout the Serra de Tramuntana. The narrow winding roads become very busy throughout the summer months making the best time to visit during the spring and autumn.

CALA SANT VICENÇ

This old-fashioned holiday resort has been given a facelift and is in danger of becoming chic. It is still very popular with Mallorcans, especially on summer weekends. Four small coves, each with its own beach, huddle together beneath Cavall Bernat, a limestone ridge which casts its shadow into the sea. A walk of around 45 minutes leads across the hills to Port de Pollença (➤ 82).

🗺 134 B3 🍴 Bars and restaurants (€–€€€) 🚌 Bus from Pollença

CAP DE FORMENTOR

See pages 26–27.

CASTELL D'ALARÓ

See pages 28–29.

COSTA NORD

The American actor Michael Douglas could be seen as a 21st-century successor to Archduke Ludwig Salvator (► 88), using his money and his influence to promote the landscapes and culture of Mallorca. In 2000 he opened Costa Nord, a multimedia cultural centre in Valldemossa devoted to Mallorca's northwest coast. The visit begins with a short film, narrated by Douglas, in which he describes his love for the island; it continues with a re-creation of the Archduke's yacht, the *Nixe*, accompanied by a commentary on his Mediterranean voyages. The shop sells a range of pricey souvenirs; there is also a café, a restaurant and a concert hall which attracts top international names during the Mediterranean Nights festival each summer. Costa Nord is a personal tribute to an island which, as Douglas says, has attracted 'poets, painters…and yes, film stars'.

➕ 132 D4 ✉ Avinguda Palma 6, Valldemossa
☎ 971 612425 🕐 Apr–Oct Tue–Sun 10–6, Mon 10–3; Nov–Mar Tue–Sun 9–5, Mon 10–3
✋ Expensive 🍴 Bar and restaurant (€€)
🚌 From Palma and Deià ❓ Mediterranean Nights, Jun–Aug

DEIÀ
See pages 34–35.

FORNALUTX
Fornalutx, in the hills above Sóller, calls itself the prettiest village in Spain, and it is hard to disagree – unless you accept the claims of its neighbour Biniaraix. There are several terrace restaurants and bars, where you can sit and soak in the views of olive and orange groves climbing ever higher until they reach the pine-clad foothills of Puig Major.
🚩 133 C6 🍴 Several restaurants (€€)

JARDINS DE ALFÁBIA
These classical gardens by the entrance to the Sóller tunnel are a legacy of the Arab talent for landscaping and irrigation. Their name derives from *al fabi*, 'jar of olives' in Arabic. They were probably designed by Benihabet, the Muslim governor of Inca who converted to Christianity following the Spanish invasion.

A flight of steps lined with tall palms leads to a covered walkway – from here you can strike off to see lily ponds, bamboo groves or citrus trees growing in the shadow of the mountains. If you have just driven over the Coll de Sóller and are in need of a rest, this would make a lovely

spot for a siesta. Take a book or some postcards, find a seat in the shade, then drift off to sleep to the sound of gently flowing water.

🚹 133 D5 ✉ Carretera Palma–Sóller, km17 ☎ 971 613123 🕓 Apr–Sep Mon–Sat 9.30–6.30; Oct–Mar Mon–Fri 9.30–5.30, Sat 9.30–1 ✋ Moderate 🍴 Ses Porxeres (€€) in the car park

LLUC
See pages 36–37.

LLUC-ALCARI
You could easily miss Mallorca's smallest village, which consists of little more than a bend in the Deià–Sóller road. With just a handful of houses and a hotel, it would make an ideal base for a walking holiday in the nearby mountains. The views are postcard-perfect – in fact you are far more likely to see it on a postcard than you are to actually go there. Picasso once lived in the village during a short stay on Mallorca.

🚹 133 D5 🚌 From Palma, Valldemossa and Port de Sóller

ORIENT

Nervous drivers should not even think about tackling the 10km (6-mile) hairpin road to Orient from Bunyola (there is a much easier approach from Alaró). But those who make it to this village are rewarded with a marvellous sight – one of Mallorca's tiniest hamlets, with a population of less than 30, nestling among olive trees at the foot of Puig d'Alfábia. Orient is popular with walkers – numerous walks start from here, including an ascent to Castell d'Alaró – and with weekend day trippers from Palma, who visit its restaurants for Sunday lunch.

🚩 133 D6 🍴 Three good restaurants (€€)

POLLENÇA

At the eastern end of the Serra de Tramuntana and tucked between two hills, each topped by a sacred site, Pollença is the perfect Mallorcan town. Large enough to avoid being twee but small enough to wander round in a morning, it has none of the feel of other towns which have succumbed under the sheer weight of tourism. Foreigners have long been attracted here, but Pollença has learned to accept and adapt to tourism without losing its soul. Café life is still the rule; if you want to join in, come on a Sunday morning when the Plaça Major is filled with market stalls and the locals congregate after church to relax in the Café Espanyol.

The Pont Romà (Roman bridge) on the edge of town gives a clue to Pollença's long history. The name Pollença dates from the 14th century, when settlers from Alcúdia named the town after their former Roman capital. Among many historic buildings is a former Jesuit convent, now the town hall. From here you climb 365 steps to the Calvari church, with its ancient wooden cross and views of Puig de Maria (▶ 96–97). The steps are the scene of a moving procession each Good Friday, when a figure of Christ is removed from a cross and carried down the steps by torchlight.

The **municipal museum** in the former Dominican convent contains the remains of prehistoric sculptures shaped like bulls, as well as a *mandala* (Tibetan sand painting) given by the Dalai Lama in 1990. The cloisters of the convent are the venue for Pollença's celebrated classical music festival.

✚ 134 B2 🍴 Excellent cafés and restaurants (€€) 🚌 From Palma
❓ Market held Sun; classical music festival, Jul–Sep; *Devallement* procession, Good Fri; *Moros i Cristians*, mock battle, 2 Aug

Museu de Pollença
✉ Carrer Guillem Cifre de Colonya ☎ 971 531166 🕐 Jul–Sep Tue–Sat 10–1, 5.30–8.30, Sun 10–1; Oct–Jun Tue–Sun 11–1 ✋ Inexpensive

PORT DE POLLENÇA

This genteel, old-fashioned resort at the mouth of Pollença bay is particularly popular with families, and with older visitors in winter. There is also a large community of foreign residents, mostly retired British. The promenade along Passeig Voramar, all whitewashed villas and pine trees leaning into the sea, is perfect for an early evening walk. Look out for the bust of Hermen Anglada-Camarasa, the Catalan painter who spent many years in Pollença and whose work is displayed in the Fundació la Caixa in Palma (➤ 48). A favourite walk from Port de Pollença is the 3km (2-mile) hike across the Formentor peninsula through the Bóquer valley, a paradise for ornithologists and lovers of wild flowers.

✚ 134 B3 🍴 Choice of restaurants (€) 🚌 From Palma, Pollença and Alcúdia; also from Port d'Alcúdia and Cap de Formentor in summer ❓ Market held Wed

PORT DE SÓLLER

This small resort, set around a fish-shaped natural harbour, has the only beach of any note along the northwest coast. It is the starting-point for several boat trips along the coast; the trip to Sa Calobra (➤ opposite) is one of the few to run throughout the year. Port de Sóller is also a good base for walks. A climb of less than an hour brings you to

Cap Gros lighthouse for panoramic views of the bay and the mountains behind; a longer path, through rock gardens and olive groves, connects with an old mule track from Deià to Sóller.

➕ 133 C5 🍴 Wide choice of restaurants (€–€€€) 🚌 From Palma, Valldemossa and Deià 🚃 From Palma; tram from Sóller

SA CALOBRA

Do not believe anyone who tells you that they have discovered the perfect unspoiled cove on the north coast – unless it's Sa Calobra. This is indeed a beautiful spot, which is why tour buses pour in by the dozen every day, even in winter.

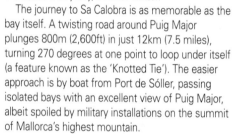

The journey to Sa Calobra is as memorable as the bay itself. A twisting road around Puig Major plunges 800m (2,600ft) in just 12km (7.5 miles), turning 270 degrees at one point to loop under itself (a feature known as the 'Knotted Tie'). The easier approach is by boat from Port de Sóller, passing isolated bays with an excellent view of Puig Major, albeit spoiled by military installations on the summit of Mallorca's highest mountain.

Once there, walk through 200m (650ft) of tunnels to reach the Torrent de Pareis ('twin streams'), which begins up in the mountains at the confluence of the torrents of Lluc and Gorg Blau. Up to 400m (1,300ft) high and only 30m (100ft) wide, with some sections never seeing daylight, this dramatic gorge culminates in a small pebble beach where you can picnic among the crowds. In summer, when the gorge is dry, you can hike inland between the cliffs; do not attempt this in winter.

A side turn off the road to Sa Calobra leads to Cala Tuent, a small cove with a sandy beach and a 13th-century church, Ermita de Sant Llorenç. Cala Tuent is likely to be quieter than Sa Calobra.

➕ 133 C6 🍴 Several restaurants (€–€€) 🚢 From Port de Sóller (all year ☎ 971 630170)

SERRA DE TRAMUNTANA

The 'mountains of the north wind' which run the length of Mallorca's northwest coast are home to the island's most spectacular landscapes. Pine-covered slopes almost lean into the sea; as you climb higher, forested hills give way to barren crags and peaks. The people of Mallorca have good reason to be grateful to the mountains. In winter they act as a buffer, shielding the plain from the fierce *tramuntana* wind and absorbing most of the island's rain and snow; in summer they provide a cool retreat from the heat of Palma and the south.

The Serra de Tramuntana for many people is the most enchanting part of the island. It runs for 88km (55 miles) from Andratx (► 60) to Pollença (► 80–81), with the rocky outcrops of Sa Dragonera (► 72) and Cap de Formentor (► 26–27) at either end. It contains Lluc, Mallorca's most sacred site (► 36–37) and Sóller, one of its prettiest villages (► 86–87).

Of the 10 peaks over 1,000m, (3,280ft) most are concentrated in the area around Lluc; the highest are Puig Major (1,445m/4,740ft) and Puig Massanella (1,349m/4,426ft). There are no rivers, though there are several mountain torrents which swell rapidly after rain – and the Cúber and Gorg Blau reservoirs, essential resources on an island so often affected by drought.

The mountains are best seen slowly, on foot; you smell the wild rosemary, hear the sheep-bells, frighten the goats, breathe in the air and marvel at pine trees growing out of red rock, a divine version of the colours of Mallorcan village houses. If you have to drive, take care – the roads here are the most dangerous on the island, and the endless procession of hairpin bends requires total concentration. The most dramatic drive of all is the C710 from Sóller to Lluc, traversing tunnels and gorges on its way between Puig Major and Puig Massanella.

✚ 132 F2–B8 ❓ Walking, birds, spring flowers

SÓLLER

Set in a lush valley of orange groves between the mountains and the sea, Sóller is popular with day trippers who arrive on the vintage train from Palma and seem to do little but sit outside the cafés in Plaça Constitució soaking up the atmosphere and the sun. With several *tapas* bars, a fine selection of pastry shops, local ice cream and freshly squeezed orange juice, there is little reason to move on.

Sóller grew rich on oranges and the results can be seen in its extravagant *modernista* architecture. The church of Sant Bartomeu has a 1912 arched tower suspended above the rose window, with spires like huge needles pointing into the air. The same architect, Gaudí's pupil Joan Rubió, designed the Banco Central Hispano next door.

A stroll to the cemetery above the station, flanked by cypress trees and filled with potted plants, gives a clue to Sóller's history.

Several of the epitaphs are in French, revealing the significant French community of the town, descendants of those who came to make their fortune by exporting oranges.

Sóller has two museums worth visiting. The **Natural Science Museum,** in a turn-of-the-19th-century manor house on the Palma road, has a collection of fossils and a botanical garden. The **Museu de Sóller** is an 18th-century town house in the town centre, filled with antiques and relics of old Sóller.

A final word of advice: come here by train, rather than car. The climb over the Coll de Sóller, with its 57 hairpin bends, is the most terrifying drive in Mallorca. There is now a controversial new road tunnel through the mountain, but the train journey from Palma is a delight so why not give yourself a treat.

➕ 133 D5 🍴 Wide choice of bars and restaurants (€–€€) 🚃 From Palma; tram to Port de Sóller ❓ Market held Sat; *Moros i Cristians*, re-enactment of a 1561 battle in which local women helped to defeat a band of Turkish pirates, 8–10 May

Natural Science Museum

✉ Carretera Palma–Port de Sóller ☎ 971 634014 🕐 Tue–Sat 10–6, Sun 10–2 💷 Inexpensive

Museu de Sóller

✉ Carrer de Sa Mar 9 ☎ 971 634663 🕐 Mon–Fri 11–4, Sat 11–1.30 ✋ Donation

SON MARROIG

Of all the famous foreigners attracted to Mallorca's northwest coast, none is so admired locally as 'S'Arxiduc', Archduke Ludwig Salvator. Born in 1847 in the Pitti Palace, Florence, the son of Leopold III of Tuscany and Marie Antoinette de Bourbon, he came to Mallorca 20 years later to escape from Viennese court life and immediately fell in love with the island. An ecologist before it was fashionable, and an early hippy who wore Mallorcan peasant clothes, he bought up estates along the coast in an effort to save them from development, and devoted himself to studying and recording Mallorcan wildlife and traditions. His seven-volume *Las Baleares* took 20 years to produce and is still an authority on its subject. He died in 1915 in a Bohemian castle.

The Archduke's home at Son Marroig, outside Deià, has been turned into a shrine to his memory, with his photographs, paintings and books and a museum devoted to his life. In the gardens is a white marble rotunda, made from Carrara marble and imported from Italy, where you can sit and gaze at the Na Foradada ('pierced rock') peninsula, jutting out to sea with a gaping 18m (59-foot) hole at its centre. Ask at the house for permission to walk onto the peninsula.

✚ 132 D4 ✉ Carretera Valldemossa– Deià ☎ 971 639158 🕐 Apr–Sep Mon–Sat 10–7.30; Oct–Mar Mon–Sat 10–5.30 ✋ Inexpensive 🍴 Mirador de Na Foradada (€€) 🚌 From Palma, Valldemossa and Port de Sóller

VALLDEMOSSA

See pages 40–41.

The Northeast

Mallorca's northeast corner has a beautiful coastline, with arguably the island's best beaches, as well as the historic towns of Alcúdia and Artà. The area is quieter than other parts of the island and attracts families to its long sandy beaches rather than the disco crowds that gather in and around Palma for the nightlife, although Port d'Alcúdia does have its share of nightspots. The dunes and marshlands including the S'Albufera wetlands (▶ 98–99) attract birdwatchers from all over Europe and the cave system at Artà is another draw to the region.

However, Artà and Alcùdia all come to life on market day when the streets are filled with people and stalls selling food, fruit, souvenirs and pottery as well as many other goods.

ALCÚDIA
See pages 22–23.

ARTÀ

Derived from the Arabic word *jertan* ('garden'), Artà has been occupied for at least 3,000 years, as evidenced by the remains of a Bronze Age site at Ses Païsses (➤ 99) just outside the town. Nowadays Artà is a prosperous little town near the coast, which gets particularly lively each Tuesday on market day.

From the parish church of Transfiguració del Senyor, an avenue of cypress trees leads to Artà's crowning glory, its hilltop fortress and Santuari de Sant Salvador. The view down over the rooftops, a jumble of tiles in every shade of brown, is one of the sights of Mallorca. On the site of a Moorish fortress, the original sanctuary walls and chapel were rebuilt in the 19th century. Walk around the battlements, rest in a peaceful courtyard, then look into the

sanctuary church with its vivid paintings of two Mallorcan heroes – Jaume the Conqueror receiving the surrender of the *walis*, and Ramón Llull being stoned to death in Tunisia. There is also a painting of Sant Antoni, patron saint of Artà, and of animals, seen here, as always, with a small pig. Each January the saint is commemorated with a masked procession and a blessing of pets. Artà's big festival, Sant Antoni de Juny, dates back to 1581 and features dancers with cardboard horses strapped to their hips.

The coastline north of Artà contains some of Mallorca's wildest and most beautiful beaches, including the virgin cove of Cala Torta.

➕ 135 E6 🍴 Several bars and restaurants (€–€€) 🚌 From Palma and Cala Rajada ❓ Market held Tue; Sant Antoni Abat, procession and blessing of pets, 16–17 Jan; Sant Antoni de Juny, *cavallets* horse dances, 13 Jun

AUTO-SAFARI (SAFARI-ZOO)

Mallorca's only zoo consists of a 4km (2.5-mile) drive through open countryside, passing giraffes, zebra, flamingos and deer (keep your car windows shut against marauding monkeys), followed by a 'baby zoo' with elephants, crocodiles and various young animals. You can also explore the 44ha (110-acre) reserve by a special 'mini-train' for which you pay a hefty supplement on top of the already considerable cost of entry.

➕ 135 F6 ✉ Carretera Porto, Cristo–Son Servera, km5 ☎ 971 810909 🕐 Apr–Sep daily 9–7; Oct–Mar daily 9–5 💷 Expensive 🍴 Café (€)

CALA MILLOR

Fifty years ago this was a
lonely dune-covered shore;
now it has become the major
resort on Mallorca's east coast. The main attraction is its fine
sandy beaches; from Cala Bona ('the good bay') to Cala Millor
('the better bay') they stretch unbroken for 2km (1.2 miles). In
summer it is 'lively', travel-agent speak for brash, and best avoided
unless you like discos and late-night bars; in winter it takes on a
new atmosphere, as a resort for the 'young at heart', another
travel-agent euphemism. To see what this coast used to be like,
walk to the headland at Punta de n'Amer (➤ 97).

✚ 135 F6 🍽 Wide choice of bars and restaurants (€–€€) 🚌 From Palma;
also from Cala Rajada and Port d'Alcúdia in summer

CALA RAJADA

This fishing port on Mallorca's eastern tip, surrounded by
fine beaches and pretty coves, is a popular summer
resort, with windsurfing, snorkelling and numerous
discos. Many Germans have second homes here.

A walk of about 2km (1.2 miles) from the harbour
leads through pine woods and crosses a headland to the
lighthouse at Punta de Capdepera, the easternmost point
on Mallorca. There are also several good beaches within
easy reach. The town beach, Son Moll, is often crowded
but for more isolation you can head north to the small cove of Cala
Gat or the broad sweep of Cala Agulla.

The other reason for coming here is to make a day trip to
Menorca (➤ 14). Boats leave each morning for the Menorcan city
of Ciutadella, with its cathedral and harbourside fish restaurants.

✚ 135 D7 🍽 Wide choice of restaurants (€€) 🚌 From Palma and Porto
Cristo; also from Cala Millor in summer ⛴ Day trips to Menorca (☎ 902
100444) ❓ Market held Sat; processions of boats, 16 July
ℹ Plaça dels Pins (☎ 971 563033)

CAPDEPERA

If you are driving between Artà and Cala Rajada, stop off to visit this small town, crowned by the largest fortress in Mallorca. The Romans were the first to build a **castle** on this site – the Moors enlarged it, the Christians destroyed it, then replaced it with one of their own in the 14th century. Legend has it that the citizens of Capdepera hid in the castle when under siege, placing an image of Our Lady of Hope on the battlements, and the invaders were driven away by fog. The miracle is recorded inside the castle in the Capella de Nostra Senyora de la Esperança and remembered each year at the town's annual *festa*. You reach the castle by climbing the steps from the market square, Plaça de l'Orient.

✚ 135 E7 🍴 Café de l'Orient, Plaça de l'Orient (€) 🚍 From Palma and Cala Rajada ❓ Market held Wed; Nostra Senyora de la Esperança *festa*, 18 Dec

Castle

☎ 971 818746 🕒 Apr–Oct daily 10–8; Nov–Mar daily 10–5 ✋ Inexpensive

COVES D'ARTÀ
See pages 32–33.

MURO

This small town between Inca and the S'Albufera marshes has one overriding attraction – the **Museu Etnòlogic de Mallorca.** Housed in a former mansion, it gives fascinating glimpses into Mallorca's past. Upstairs there is a fine collection of *siurells* (clay whistles) featuring men on horseback, carrying water and playing guitars. A courtyard with a well, a waterwheel and orange trees leads to more exhibits – blacksmith's and cobbler's workshops, a collection of carriages, and tools once used by silversmiths, sculptors and spoonmakers.

The Catalan-Gothic church of Sant Joan Baptista looks almost Arabic, guarded by palm trees and a tall, square bell-tower linked to the main church by a tiny bridge. Rebuilt in the 16th century, it has a colourful rose window over the west door. Another church, the convent of Santa Anna, used to stage fights between bulls and bulldogs, and bullfights can still be seen at the Plaça de Toros, built out of white stone in its own quarry in 1910.

Sa Pobla, 4km (2.5 miles) north of Muro, is Mallorca's vegetable basket; this fertile area of marshes reclaimed as farmland is referred to as 'the land of a thousand windmills'. It is also the home of one of Mallorca's most unusual festivals, the Revelta de Sant Antoni. For two days each January pets are led through the town to be blessed outside the church, dancers drive out the Devil for the coming year, and everyone eats pastries filled with spicy spinach and marsh eels.

➕ 134 D3 ❓ Sun market; Revelta de Sant Antoni, 16–17 Jan 🚂 Train from Palma

Museu Etnòlogic de Mallorca
✉ Carrer Major 15 ☎ 971 717540 🕐 Tue–Wed, Fri–Sat 10–3, Thu 10–7, Sun 10–2 ✋ Inexpensive

PORT D'ALCÚDIA

As the name suggests, this was once just a port serving a city – now the port has completely outgrown the town that it serves. The biggest of the resorts on Mallorca's northeast coast, it stands at the head of a 10km (6-mile) stretch of sandy beach which continues around the bay of Alcúdia as far as Can Picafort. The area around the fishing harbour is the most attractive; the promenade on Passeig Marítim faces a row of fish restaurants. Near here is the commercial port, where passenger ferries leave for the Menorcan city of Ciutadella.

✚ 134 C4 🍴 Wide choice of restaurants (€€) 🚌 From Palma and Alcúdia; also from Port de Pollença in summer

PUIG DE MARIA

Climb for an hour out of Pollença, or drive up a terrifying potholed road, and you are rewarded with views over Cap de Formentor and the entire northeastern coast – as well as back down over Pollença. Nuns settled on Puig de Maria ('Mary's mountain') in 1371 and remained for several hundred years, refusing to leave even when the Bishop of Palma ordered them down for their own safety. The convent is still there, on top of the mountain; the chapel smells of incense

and the refectory of woodsmoke. You can stay in simple cells in the sanctuary here, but don't expect luxury – unless you count waking to a view of sunrise over Pollença Bay.

The caretaker will rustle up a *paella* to save you the long walk back to town.

✚ 134 B2 ☎ 971 184132 🍴 Bar-restaurant (€) 🚌 From Palma to Pollença ✋ Free

PUNTA DE N'AMER

This 200ha (495-acre) nature reserve on a headland jutting out from the east coast is an oasis of peace amid a desert of high-rise apartments and hotels. Once, the whole coast was like this – thankfully, environmentalists have saved this small section from development. Walk south from Cala Millor, or north from Sa Coma, on a well-defined 1.5km (1-mile) track. Eventually you reach the Castell de n'Amer, a 17th-century watchtower. Have a drink at the summit and look down at what you have left behind.

✚ 135 F7 🍴 Snack bar (€) 🚌 From Palma to Cala Millor ✋ Free

S'ALBUFERA

Just off the coast road 5km (3 miles) south of Port d'Alcúdia, the Parc Natural de S'Albufera wetlands make a welcome relief from long stretches of crowded beach. Birdwatchers come from all over Europe to see rare migrants like Montagu's harriers and Eleanora's falcons; species breeding here include stonechats, moustached warblers and the long-eared owl. Ospreys leave their breeding sites on the cliffs to come here to fish; peregrines and hoopoes live here all year round.

The name derives from the Arabic for 'lagoon', but the site has been exploited since Roman times – Pliny writes of night herons, probably from S'Albufera, being sent to Rome as a gastronomic delicacy. The wetlands were drained for agriculture in the 19th century by a British company which subsequently went bankrupt; the network of canals dates from this time. Rice was introduced in the early 20th century, paper was manufactured from the reeds and sedge, and it is only since 1985, following fears that tourist development was damaging the area's fragile ecology, that S'Albufera has been a protected nature reserve. There are

footpaths, cycle trails, bird-watching hides and audiovisual display room where you can listen to birdsong.

🚩 134 D3 ✉ Carretera Port d'Alcúdia–Artà, km5 ☎ 971 892250 🕓 Apr–Sep daily 9–6; Oct–Mar daily 9–5 🍴 Picnic area 🚌 From Port d'Alcúdia to Cala Rajada in summer 🎟 Free ❓ Cars not allowed in the reserve – leave them 1km (0.5 miles) from the visitor centre on the main road in the car park opposite Hotel Parc Natural

SES PAÏSSES

Although not as extensive as the ruins at Capocorb Vell (➤ 106–107), this Bronze Age settlement near Artà is still a significant site and a link with Mallorcans of 3,000 years ago. Most impressive of all is the massive entrance portal, formed from three stone slabs weighing up to eight tonnes each. Inside there are several rooms and an *atalaia* (watchtower); the entire settlement is surrounded by a Cyclopean drystone wall.

🚩 135 E6 🕓 Apr–Oct Mon–Sat 9.30–1, 4–7.30; Nov–Mar Mon–Fri 9–1, 2–5 🎟 Inexpensive 🚌 From Cala Rajada or Palma then short walk

Inland, East and the South

The rural heartland of Mallorca lies to the south and is seemingly untouched by the tourist invasions of the coastal towns further north. Agricultural activity dominates the area and there is no more impressive a sight than the blanket of pretty white almond blossom that carpets the countryside in February each year. The flat plain, *Es Pla*, is a patchwork of orchards and almond groves with some hills dotted here and there where you will find villages and towns of the 'real Mallorca'. This area attracts a lot of investment from foreign buyers, and some country hotels are springing up, but for the most part the area remains unspoiled and a peaceful place to wander along the country lanes that were laid down in Roman times.

On the southeast coast there are some busy resorts such as Cala d'Or, with Porto Cristo on the east coast, but the coastline is quite rugged and some of the beaches and coves are only accessible by boat. Further offshore the island of Cabrera is home to a wide range of seabirds and wildlife including Mediterranean turtles.

Inset map: *Illa de Cabrera*

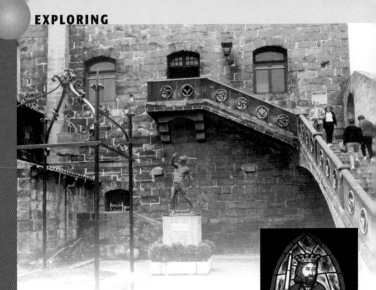

ALGAIDA

Algaida is a typical Mallorcan town, all green shutters, narrow streets, a square lined with cafés and a huge sandstone church. Few visitors make it into the town centre; the attractions are all on the outskirts, on the Palma–Manacor road. The main one is **Ca'n Gordiola**, a glass factory in a mock castle. The ground floor contains a workshop (though it looks more like a church with its arches and stained glass) where you can watch glass being blown; upstairs there is a museum devoted to the history of glass making. A further 2km (1.2 miles) along the road to Manacor is a string of well-known restaurants, where the people of Palma head at weekends for old-fashioned Mallorcan cuisine.

🔢 137 B7 🍴 Restaurants on the Palma–Manacor road (€) 🚌 From Palma
❓ Market held Fri

Ca'n Gordiola

✉ Carretera Palma–Manacor, km19 ☎ 971 665046 🕐 Apr–Oct Mon–Sat 9–7.30, Sun 9–12; Nov–Mar Mon–Sat 9–1.30, 3–7, Sun 9–12 💷 Free

BINISSALEM

If you order Mallorcan wine in a restaurant, it will probably come from Binissalem. Viticulture was introduced here by the Romans and has survived in much reduced form. The reputation of Binissalem red wines, made with the local grape Manto Negro, has been growing recently – the best-known *bodega*, José L Ferrer, offering tastings and guided tours, is on the right as you enter the town from Palma. Binissalem is a handsome town with a well-preserved old quarter in the streets around the church square.

➕ 133 E7 🍴 Several restaurants and bars (€€) 🚆 Train from Palma and Inca ❓ Market held Fri; wine festival last weekend in Sep

CABRERA, ILLA DE

'Goat island' is the largest in a rocky archipelago 10km (6 miles) off the south coast. Pliny claimed it as the birthplace of Hannibal and during the Napoleonic Wars it became a notorious prison camp. Since 1991 the island has been a protected national park. You can only get there on a day trip by boat, with time to walk up to the 14th-century castle above the harbour, visit a museum in an old wine cellar and swim in the Blue Grotto on the way back.

➕ 136 F2 (inset) 🚢 From Colònia de Sant Jordi, Apr–Oct daily 9.30 (☎ 971 649034)

CALA D'OR

Each of the various *calas* (bays) along the east coast has its own distinctive character; in the case of Cala d'Or the word is 'chic'. Former fishing harbours have been turned into marinas; people come here to sail and dive, and drink champagne at waterfront bars. The villas are white and flat-roofed, in Ibizan style, designed in the 1930s by Pep Costa Ferrer, and the effect is surprisingly attractive.

Nowadays Cala d'Or is the collective name for a string of resorts, beaches and coves; they include Porto Petro, around a horseshoe bay 2km (1.2 miles) to the south, and Cala Mondragó, a further 4km (2.5 miles) south, where a pair of sandy beaches form part of the Mondragó nature reserve.

➕ 139 E5 🍴 Wide choice of restaurants (€€–€€€) 🚌 From Palma

CALA FIGUERA

More than anywhere else in Mallorca, Cala Figuera retains the atmosphere of a working fishing port. White-painted houses reach down to the water's edge and fishermen sit on the steps mending nets. If you get here early enough in the morning you might even see the catch coming in. A path follows around the tiny harbour and onto the cliffs, offering good views back towards the bay. The nearest beach is 4km (2.5 miles) to the south at Cala Santanyí.

✚ 138 E4

🍴 Several seafood restaurants and others (€€)
🚌 From Palma and Santanyí

CAMPOS

Midway from Llucmajor to Santanyí on the C717, Campos was founded by Jaume II in 1300 on the site of earlier Roman and Arab settlements. A painting of Christ by the Sevillian artist Murillo hangs in the **parish church of Sant Julià.** Next door to the church is a museum with a large collection of offertory bowls. To visit both the church and the museum, meet the parish priest

outside the church door at 11am for a guided tour. Campos has a busy market on Thursdays and Saturdays and its port adjoins the resort of Colònia de Sant Jordi (➤ 107) to the south.

✚ 138 D2 🍴 Several cafés and bars (€) 🚌 From Palma

Església de Sant Julià
✉ Carrer Bisbe Talladas 17 ☎ 971 650003 ◷ Mon–Sat 11am 🖐 Donation

CAPOCORB VELL

These are the most significant remains of the Talaiotic culture, which flourished in Mallorca between around 1300 and 800BC. Villages were dominated by *talaiots*, circular or rectangular structures two to three storeys high, which were used as both burial chambers and defensive forts. Each settlement was surrounded by Cyclopean walls, built from massive, unhewn stones without mortar to hold them together. There is no evidence of a written language, so the stones are all that archaeologists have to go on in understanding prehistoric Mallorcan culture. At Capocorb Vell, 12km (7.5 miles) south of Llucmajor, you can see five *talaiots* and wander around the ancient village, 100m (330ft) above sea level just inland from the coast. The Talaiotic people kept sheep, and the sound of sheep bells in the nearby fields is a touching reminder of continuity.

🔒 137 D6 ✉ Carretera Cap Blanc–Llucmajor
☎ 971 180155 🕐 Fri–Wed 10–5 👑 Inexpensive
🍴 Nearby (€)

COLÒNIA DE SANT JORDI

Once the port for the market town of Campos, Colònia de Sant Jordi is now a busy resort, on a rocky promontory close to Mallorca's southern tip. Its small beach looks out over several islets, with good views all the way to Cabrera (➤ 103). There are two further sandy beaches to the east, and the long stretch of Platja Es Trenc begins just west of town. To the north are the hot springs of Banys de Sant Joan. The main reason for coming here, though, is to take the boat trip to Cabrera.

🔒 138 E2 🍴 Choice of restaurants (€–€€€)
🚌 From Palma ❓ Market held Wed

COVES DEL DRAC

Dank, dark and humid, the limestone Dragon Caves on the edge of Porto Cristo have become one of Mallorca's top tourist sights. Groups of several hundred people at a time are herded along 2km (1.2 miles) of slippery paths by guides who tell you in four languages how to interpret the bizarre stalactite formations – a cactus here, a flag there, the Fairies' Theatre, Diana's Bath…. You might just think they resemble thousands of spiky parsnips hanging from the ceiling. Try to imagine how Walt Disney would conjure up a fabulous witches' cave and you have the idea. The one-hour tour ends with a floodlit, floating violin concert on Lake Martel, Europe's largest underground lake, named in honour of the French geologist Édouard Martel who first explored these caves in the late 19th century at the commission of Archduke Ludwig Salvator. Afterwards you can return by boat across the lake to the exit.

✚ 139 B6 ☎ 971 820753 🕐 Apr–Oct, tours on the hour 10–5; Nov–Mar, tours at 10.45, 12, 2, 3.30 ✋ Expensive 🍴 Café (€) 🚌 From Palma and Cala Rajada

COVES DELS HAMS

You cannot miss these caves as you drive from Manacor to Porto Cristo. Most people only want to visit one set of caves and the giant billboards and flags at the entrance are an attempt to ensure that this is the one. In fact you are better off continuing to the Coves del Drac (➤ above) or up the coast to the Coves d'Artà (➤ 32–33).

But for serious speleologists, here are the facts. The caves were discovered by Pedro Caldentey in 1905 and the electric lighting was added by his son. Their name means 'fish-hooks', which the stalactites are said to resemble. You get a guided tour and, yes, another concert on an underground lake.

✚ 139 B6 ✉ Carretera Manacor–Porto Cristo ☎ 971 820988 🕐 Apr–Oct daily 10–6; Nov–Mar daily 10.30–5 ✋ Expensive 🍴 Café-restaurant (€)

ERMITA DE BONANY

This hilltop hermitage is where Junípero Serra preached his last sermon in Mallorca before leaving to found the Mexican and Californian missions. The views from the terrace, covering almost the entire plain, are superb. You can stay here in simple cells, but unlike other monasteries it has no restaurant or bar – just a chapel and a small shop selling religious trinkets.

✚ 138 B3 ☎ 971 561101
🖐 Free

FELANITX

Felanitx is at the centre of Mallorca's second wine-producing area and it is also known for its capers, or 'green pearls'. You can buy them at the Sunday morning market, in the streets around the church of Sant Miquel, with local pottery displayed on the church steps. The church façade contains a memorial to 414 people who died when a wall collapsed in 1844; further up, beneath the rose window, is the archangel Michael standing on the Devil's head.

➕ 138 C4 🍴 Bars and cafés (€) 🚌 From Palma and Porto Colom ❓ Market held Sun; Sant Agusti, *cavallets* horse dances, 28 Aug

INCA

Mallorca's third-largest town styles itself 'city of leather', and if you come on an organized tour you will undoubtedly be taken to a leather factory. Shop around; the bargains these days are few and far between. It's better to come on Thursdays, when the streets around Plaça d'Espanya are taken over by Mallorca's largest weekly market. There's plenty of leather here, of varying quality, plus jewellery, carved olive-wood, lace and fresh produce from across the island.

Plaça d'Espanya itself becomes an open-air flower show. Near here are a smart coffee-house, Café Mercantil, with upholstered leather chairs, and Ca'n Delante (✉ Carrer Major 27), one of Mallorca's top pastry shops. Inca is also known for its *cellers*, old wine-cellars turned into restaurants featuring traditional dishes at reasonable prices.

➕ 133 D7 🍴 Wide choice of restaurants (€) 🚌 From Palma 🚂 From Palma

LLUCMAJOR

This ordinary country town, the largest in southern Mallorca, has a place in history – it was the site of the battle in 1349 where Pedro IV of Aragón killed his relative Jaume III to end Mallorca's brief spell as an independent kingdom. Jaume's death is commemorated by a statue at the end of Passeig Jaume III. Near by, on Carrer Obispo Taxaquet, is another statue in honour of Llucmajor's cobblers. Shoemaking is still a significant industry here. Almonds and apricots grow around the town and make good buys at the market, held twice a week in Plaça d'Espanya.

🚻 137 C7 🍴 Cafés and bars (€) 🚌 From Palma
❓ Market held Wed, Sun

MANACOR

Mallorca's second city is the nearest thing the island has to an industrial town. Despite the lack of obvious sights, the narrow streets behind the church make a pleasant place to stroll and soak up the atmosphere of everyday Mallorca. The church, Església dels Delors de Nostra Senyora, was built on the site of a mosque and its minaret-style tower can be seen for miles. Look inside to see the figure of Christ with scrawny hair and a skirt – pilgrims queue up to kiss his bloodstained feet.

Almost every visitor to Manacor ends up at a pearl factory – **Perlas Majórica** is the best-known. Mallorca's artificial pearl industry produces 50 million pearls a year, using the scales of a million fish, so do not imagine they

are a safe alternative for your vegetarian friends. They are said to be indistinguishable from the real thing, and almost as expensive.

➕ 138 B4 🍴 Several bars and cafés (€) 🚌 From Palma and Porto Cristo ❓ Market held Mon

Perlas Majórica

✉ Avinguda Majórica 48 ☎ 971 550200 🕐 Mon–Fri 9–7, Sat–Sun 10–1 ♿ Free

MONTUÏRI

High on a ridge surrounded by old stone windmills, the village of Montuïri is probably the most impressive sight along the Palma–Manacor road. The eight mill-towers of the Molinar district, redundant since the 1920s, are the symbol of the village; the best views are from the Ermita de Sant Miquel, a 19th-century hermitage on top of a small hill 2km (1.2 miles) to the east. Montuïri is the setting for one of Mallorca's most spectacular festivals: each August *Cossiers*, accompanied by dancers with bagpipes, flutes and drums, dress up as women and devils and perform a dance, the origins of which stretch back at least 400 years, where evil is overcome by good.

➕ 138 B2 🍴 Bars and restaurants (€) 🚌 From Palma ❓ Market on Mon; Sant Bartomeu festival, 24 Aug; Fira de la Perdiu (partridge and hunting fair), first Sun in Dec

PETRA

This sleepy town of sand-coloured houses would be completely off the tourist map if it were not the birthplace of Mallorca's most famous son, Fray Junípero Serra. Born in 1713, he became a priest in 1730 and worked as a missionary in Mexico from 1749 to 1763. At the age of 54 he was sent to California; the missions he established there grew into some of the USA's largest cities, including San Diego and San Francisco.

You can visit the **house** where Serra's parents lived, a **museum** devoted to his life and work, the nearby San Bernardino convent where he went to school and a plaque, outside the parish church, describing him as 'explorer, missionary, hero, civiliser'. Anyone walking down the street leading to his birthplace, decorated with majolica tiles depicting him baptizing Native Americans, might be inclined to disagree, but by the standards of his day he was certainly a hero.

✚ 138 A3 🍴 Es Celler restaurant (€€); bars on main square (€) 🚂 Train from Palma ❓ Market held Wed

Serra House and Museum

✉ Carrer Barracar Alt ☎ 971 561149 🕐 By arrangement – follow the directions to the keyholder's house ✋ Donation requested

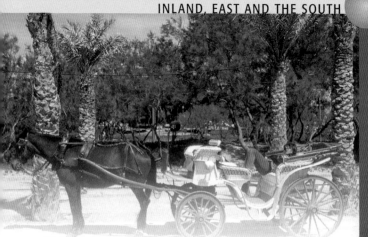

PLATJA DE PALMA

This 5km (3-mile) stretch of fine white sand is just minutes from the airport. The two resorts of Can Pastilla and S'Arenal have merged into one, connected by a palm-lined promenade. It's a good resort for families – there are children's playgrounds and a miniature train ride, though the nightlife can get a bit raucous. Take a *passeig* (promenade) here before dinner and you will have a fabulous view of the twinkling lights of Palma.

✚ 137 C5 🍴 Bars and restaurants (€–€€) 🚌 Regular buses from Palma

PORRERES

Porreres is typical of the small towns on the Mallorcan plain – nothing much to see, but an easy-going atmosphere and a good place to while away a couple of hours. The main street, Avinguda Bisbe Campins, runs from the church to the town hall and is lined with bars and cafés. A former hospital contains the **Museu i Fons Artistic,** with works by Salvador Dalí. Outside town is a former hilltop hermitage, Santuari de Montesió, with a simple chapel, irregular cloisters and views across the plain and out to sea.

✚ 138 C2 🍴 Choice of restaurants and bars (€) ❓ Market held Tue

Museu i Fons Artistic

✉ Carrer Reverend Agustí Font 23 ☎ 971 647221 🕐 Tue, Sat 11–2; also temporary exhibitions Fri–Sun 7pm–9pm 💷 Free

a drive around the Central Plain

This lovely drive criss-crosses the central plain (Es Pla), following old Roman roads through almond and apricot groves and vineyards on its way to a number of small market towns.

Start in Petra by the parish church, following signs to Felanitx. On the way out of the village, you pass the road leading up to Ermita de Bonany (➤ 110), where the views are splendid across the plain.

Keep straight ahead at a roundabout to cross over the C715, the main road from Palma to Manacor. Stay on this country road for 7km (4 miles), then turn left towards Felanitx (➤ 110–111). When you see the town ahead of you, take a sharp right turn, signposted to Porreres.

Follow this road across fertile countryside for 12km (7.5 miles) and into the centre of Porreres (➤ 115), which is

a good place to stop for lunch with its numerous bars and cafés.

Leaving Porreres, follow signs to Llucmajor. Stay on this road for 12km (7.5 miles) as farmland gradually gives way to woods. Reaching Llucmajor (► 112) – with its Wednesday and Saturday market – turn left at the roundabout and stay on the ring road to the far end of town; turn right, following signs to Algaida.

The road rises and falls for 8km (5 miles) around the foot of Puig de Randa (► 121–121), a highlight of Mallorca with its sense of history and religious connotations. When you reach Algaida (► 102), turn right to briefly join the C715 to Manacor. After 1km (0.5 miles), turn left towards Pina and stay on this rural road through Pina and Lloret de Vista Alegre, with views of the sierra in the distance as you head for Sineu (► 125). Here you can visit the modern art gallery, S'Estació, in an old station.

Just before entering Sineu (come on a Wednesday morning for one of Mallorca's most traditional markets), turn right to skirt the town centre and turn right again to return to Petra on the old road.

Distance 80km (50 miles)
Time 2 hours
Start/end point Petra ✚ 138 A3
Lunch Centro (€) ✉ Avinguda Bisbe Campins, Porreres
☎ 971 168372

PORTO COLOM

This fishing village, once the port for Felanitx, was named in honour of Christopher Columbus, who is said – without much evidence – to have been born here. Until the late 19th century Porto Colom was busy supplying wine to France; but when phylloxera killed the vines, its role as a port diminished and it has only recently discovered a new life as a tourist resort. Popular with Mallorcan and Spanish visitors and set inside a deep natural harbour, it still has the feel of a small fishing port with boats around the quay and pastel-coloured houses lining the waterfront, each with its own landing stage. Cala Marçal, 2km (1.2 miles) south, has a wide sandy beach leading to a narrow rocky cove.

🚹 139 D5 🍴 Choice of restaurants (€€) 🚌 From Palma and Felanitx

PORTO CRISTO

This was one of the main resorts on the east coast until Cala Millor came along. So much the better: with bigger and better beaches elsewhere, Porto Cristo has carved out a role as a friendly, family resort, taking advantage of a superb position at the end of a long, sheltered inlet. Once the port for Manacor, Porto Cristo was the only place in Mallorca to be caught up in the Spanish Civil War, when it was briefly captured by Republican forces in 1936. There is not much to do but swim, sunbathe and dine at the terrace restaurants which are perfectly placed to catch the lunchtime sun – but day trippers come in droves to visit the nearby Coves del Drac (➤ 108). Other nearby family attractions include an aquarium.

➕ 139 B6 🍴 Wide choice of restaurants (€€) 🚌 From Palma and Manacor ❓ Market held Sun

PÒRTOL

The neighbouring villages of Pòrtol and Sa Cabaneta, between Palma and Santa María del Camí, have become something of an artists' colony. Unlike in Deià and Banyalbufar, though, the artists are Mallorcan – potters taking advantage of the rich local soil. The only reason for coming here is to visit the *ollerías* (workshops), where prices are much lower than in the tourist shops. Good buys include *greixoneras* (heavy earthenware cooking pots) and *ollas* (clay storage jars), as well as simple brown-glazed plates and *plats morenos*, glazed bowls painted with symbols (some of the designs go back to Arab times). Several artists specialize in the miniature earthenware figures known as *siurells*, which incorporate a crude whistle in the base.

➕ 137 A6 🍴 Bars (€) 🚌 From Palma ❓ Market held Thu; Fira del Fang, annual pottery fair held in Mar in the nearby town of Marratxí

PUIG DE RANDA

This table mountain, rising 540m (1,771ft) out of the plain, has been a place of pilgrimage ever since Ramón Llull founded Mallorca's first hermitage here in 1275. He came aged 40, shaken by an incident which caused him to review his way of life. Bent on seduction he chased a married woman through Palma on horseback; unable to shake him off, she lifted her blouse to reveal cancerous breasts. Llull retired in isolation to Puig de Randa to ponder a life of youthful excess. These days pilgrims to Puig de Randa are as likely to be weekend cyclists in search of a challenge as seekers after religious truth.

The winding road to the summit leads to three separate hermitages. The lowest, Oratori de Nostra Senyora de Gràcia, is perched on a ledge in the cliff above a sheer 200m (655ft) drop. Further up is the Santuari de Sant Honorat and finally Santuari de Cura, where Llull lived. The sense of history is somewhat offset by the radio mast on the mountain top and the electric candles in the church, but this is still a special place. Visit the Sala Gramàtica to see Llull's original manuscripts and a bottle of 1934 Chartreuse

made in the monastery, then look out from the terrace at the views of the plain, with Palma Bay and the isle of Cabrera in the distance. Simple rooms are available if you want to stay the night.

➕ 137 C8 ☎ 971 120260 🖐 Free 🍴 Restaurant at Santuari de Cura (€€)

SANTA EUGÈNIA

People argue over whether the mountains or the coast represent 'the real Mallorca', but the heart of the island is to be found in villages like this, surrounded by farmland with views to where the mountains rise out of the plain. The 6km (4-mile) cart track to the neighbouring village of Sencelles offers good walking, and there is also the climb to Puig de Santa Eugènia. Natura Parc, on the edge of the village, is a popular family attraction with nature trails and indigenous farm animals as well as a butterfly garden.

➕ 137 A7 🍴 Local bars (€) 🚌 One or two buses daily from Palma
❓ Market held Sat

SANTA MARÍA DEL CAMÍ

This market town on the Palma–Inca railway has developed a reputation as one of Mallorca's artistic centres. Most of the island's potters work close by, in Pòrtol (➤ 119), and Santa María is the centre of manufacture of *roba de llengues* ('cloth of tongues'), cotton woven into bright zigzag patterns and used in curtains, bedspreads and upholstery. Just off the main square is Ca'n Conrado, former Carmelite cloisters and a peaceful retreat from the traffic on the Palma road.

➕ 137 A6 🍴 Bars and cafés (€) 🚃 From Palma and Inca ❓ Market Sun

SANTANYÍ

Do not be surprised if the buildings in Santanyí look just that little bit more mellow than everywhere else – this small town is the source of the golden sandstone used in Palma's cathedral and La Llotja among others. The old gate, Sa Porta Murada, seen as you

enter the town from Palma, is a good example of Santanyí stone and a reminder that this was once a walled town. The parish church of Sant Andreu Apòstel contains a massive rococo organ, designed by Jordi Bosch and brought here from a convent in Palma. The streets around the church are the focus for one of Mallorca's liveliest markets.

✚ 138 E3 🍴 Bars and cafés (€) 🚌 From Palma and Cala Figuera ❓ Market held Wed, Sat; Sant Andreu *festa*, 30 Nov

SANTUARI DE SANT SALVADOR

This old hermitage, 509m (1,670ft) above sea level at the highest point of the Serra de Llevant, was the senior house of Mallorca's monastic order and the last to lose its monks, in 1992. It is still a popular place of pilgrimage, flanked by two enormous landmarks – to one side a 14m (643ft) stone cross, to the other a 35m (115ft) column topped by a statue of Christ holding out his right hand in blessing. The church contains a fine carved alabaster retable, but more interesting is the side chapel off the gatehouse, full of poignant mementoes and prayers to Our Lady. Like other former

monasteries, Sant Salvador has a few simple rooms available for pilgrims.

The views from the terrace take in Cabrera, Cap de Formentor and several other hilltop sanctuaries dotted across the plain. From the statue of Christ you look out towards the Castell de Santueri, a 14th-century rock castle built into the cliffs on the site of a ruined Arab fortress.

✚ 138 D4 ✉ Signposted from Felanitx–Porto Colom road ☎ 971 827282 ⚹ Free ⁌ Bar-restaurant (€) and picnic tables

SES COVETES

The name of this village means 'small caves' and this is believed to refer to Roman burial chambers on the same site. Nowadays people come here for one thing – to get to Platja Es Trenc, a 3km (2-mile) stretch of fine white sand backed by gentle dunes. This has long been an unofficial nudist beach, even during the puritanical Franco era. It no longer has the hippy atmosphere of old, but it still makes a peaceful, less commercial contrast to some of the other beaches on the south coast.

✚ 138 E2 🚌 From Palma, Jul–Aug, three times a day

SES SALINES

This small town between Santanyí and Colònia de Sant Jordi is named after the nearby saltpans, which act as a magnet for migrant waders and wildfowl on their way from Africa to their breeding grounds in Europe each spring. Cap de Ses Salines, Mallorca's southernmost point, is another good spot for birdwatching. The town itself makes a pleasant place to stroll, with an abundance of local Santanyí sandstone which turns golden in the sun.

Just outside Ses Salines, on the road to Santanyí, is **Botanicactus,** one of Europe's largest botanical gardens, with bamboo and palm trees and, extraordinarily diverse in form, dozens of varieties of cactus.

➕ 138 E3 🍽 Bars and cafés (€) 🚌 Between Colònia de Sant Jordi and Santanyí ❓ Market held Thu

Botanicactus

✉ Carretera Ses Salines– Santanyí, km1 ☎ 971 649494 ✇ Jun–Sep daily 9–7.30; Oct–May daily 9–5 ✋ Moderate

SINEU

Sineu, at the geographical centre of Mallorca, comes alive each Wednesday morning at the island's most traditional market. It takes place on several levels. The sound of bleating leads you to the livestock market, where weather-beaten farmers haggle over the price of sheep before heading for the town's *celler* restaurants for an early brunch. Further up, on the way to the church, you pass the symbol of Sineu, a winged lion; near here are numerous stalls selling leather, lace and pearls. Eventually you reach Sa Plaça, the church square, where the action is liveliest of all, as local housewives turn out to buy the week's food. Buckets of olives, strings of tomatoes, bags of squirming snails – they are all here, along with plenty of fresh fruit, vegetables and flowers. Get to Sineu early, before the tour buses arrive, to catch the flavour of a traditional country market. Good buys include dried figs and apricots, pottery from Pòrtol and baskets from Sudan. Also in Sineu is **S'Estació,** an unusual modern art gallery based in the old station.

🚩 138 A2 🍴 Several restaurants (€€) 🚌 From Palma ❓ Market held Wed

S'Estació

✉ Carrer Estació 2 ☎ 971 520750 🕐 Mon–Fri 9.30–1.30, 4–7, Sat 9.30–1 ✋ Free

VILAFRANCA DE BONANY

As you drive through this small town on the old road from Palma to Manacor, you cannot help noticing the strings of vegetables hanging outside several of the shops – peppers, aubergines, garlic and, above all, tomatoes. These are the famous *tomàtigues de ramallet*, sold on their stalks to be spread over *pa amb oli*. Vilafranca is also known for its honeydew melons, whose harvest is celebrated with a large melon festival each September. The other reason for coming here, apart from food, is to visit **Els Calderers,** a manor house between Vilafranca and Sant Joan. This was once at the centre of a great wine estate but like so many others it fell victim to the phylloxera disease. Reopened in 1993, the 18th-century house is now a museum of Mallorcan furniture and traditions; you can visit the wine cellar, granary, bakery, chapel and wash-house as well as wander around the main house with its paintings, guns and hunting trophies.

✚ 138 B3 🚌 From Palma and Manacor ❓ Market held Wed

Els Calderers

✉ Carretera Palma–Manacor, km37 ☎ 971 526069 🕐 Apr–Sep daily 10–6; Oct–Mar daily 10–5 💷 Expensive 🍴 Café (€)

Index

Acknowledgements

The Automobile Association would like to thank the following photographers and companies for their assistance in the preparation of this book.

Abbreviations for the picture credits are as follows – (t) top; (b) bottom; (c) centre; (l) left; (r) right; (AA) AA World Travel Library

4l Tram in Soller, AA/P Baker; **4c** Deia, AA/P Baker; **4r** View over Palma from Castell de Bellver, AA/P Baker; **5l** Cala Figuera, AA/P Baker; **5c** Restaurant, Valldemossa, AA/C Sawyer; **6/7** Tram, Soller, AA/P Baker; **10** Flamenco show, AA/K Paterson; **13** Ferries, Palma, AA/C Sawyer; **14** Excursion boat, AA/C Sawyer; **14/15** Road, Orient, AA/C Sawyer; **16** Policeman, AA/C Sawyer; **18/19** Policeman, AA/C Sawyer; **20/21** Deia, AA/P Baker; **22** Porta del Moll, AA/J Cowham; **22/23** Roman Pollentia, AA/C Sawyer; **23** Porta del Moll, AA/C Sawyer; **24/25t** Portals Vells, AA/K Paterson; **24/25b** Magaluf, AA/K Paterson; **26** Cap de Formentor, AA/K Paterson; **26/27** Cap de Formentor, AA/P Baker; **28** Castell d'Alaro, AA/K Paterson; **28/29** Castell d'Alaro, AA/P Baker; **30** Castell de Bellver, AA/K Paterson; **30/31** Castell de Bellver, AA/J Cowham; **31** Castell de Bellver, AA/C Sawyer; **32/33** Arta cave, AA/K Paterson; **33** View from Arta cave, AA/P Baker; **34** Deia, AA/W Voysey; **34/35** Deia AA/K Paterson; **35b** Window in Deia, AA/K Paterson; **36** Chapel at Lluc, AA/K Paterson; **36/37t** Virgin statue at Lluc, AA/K Paterson; **36/37b** Monastery at Lluc, AA/K Paterson; **38** Palma Cathedral, AA/K Paterson; **38/39** Palma Cathedral, AA/K Paterson; **39** Palma Cathedral interior, AA/K Paterson; **40** Monastery at Valldemossa, AA/K Paterson; **40/41t** Market in Valldemossa, AA/K Paterson; **41** George Sand portrait, Valldemossa, AA/P Baker; **42/43** View from Castell de Bellver over Palma, AA/P Baker; **45** Flower stall, Palma, AA/P Baker; **46** Arab Baths, Palma, AA/P Baker; **47** Statue of Junipero Serra, Palma, AA/P Baker; **48** Fundacio la Caixa, Palma, AA/K Paterson; **48/49** Fundacio Miro, Palma, AA/P Baker; **50** Can Corbella, Palma, AA/C Sawyer; **50/51b** Placa Cort, Palma, AA/K Paterson; **51** Statue of Jaume I of Aragon, Palma, AA/K Paterson; **52** Mercat Olivar, Palma, AA/P Baker; **53** Fundacion Juan March, Palma, AA/K Paterson; **54cl** Palau de L'Almundaina, Palma, AA/K Paterson; **54tr** Museu de Mallorca, Palma, AA/K Paterson; **55** Palau de L'Almundaina, Palma, AA/K Paterson; **56/57** Palau March Museum, AA/C Sawyer; **57** Passeig des Born, Palma, AA/P Baker; **58** Poble Espanyol, Palma, AA/P Baker; **59** Puigpunyent, AA/K Paterson; **60/61** Andratx, AA/P Baker; **61b** Banyalbufar, AA/P Baker; **62** La Granja, AA/K Paterson; **62/63** Watchtower, Estellencs, AA/P Baker; **63tr** View near Estellencs, AA/K Paterson; **64** Tiles, Calvia, AA/K Paterson; **65** Galilea, AA/K Paterson; **66t** Dancing, La Granja, AA/K Paterson; **66b** Potter, La Granja, AA/K Paterson; **67** Grounds of La Granja, AA/K Paterson; **68/69t** Magaluf, AA/ Paterson; **68/69b** Palma Nova, AA/J Cowham; **70** Port d'Antratx, AA/K Paterson; **70/71** Portals Vells, AA/K Paterson; **72** La Reserva, AA/K Paterson; **72/73** View to Sa Dragonera, AA/K Paterson; **73b** Sa Dragonera, AA/K Paterson; **74** Relief on cross depicting Jaume I, Santa Ponca, AA/W Voysey; **75** Cala Barques, Cala Sant Vicenc, AA/J Cowham; **76/77** Cala Sant Vicenc, AA/P Baker; **78** Fornalutx, AA/P Baker; **78/79** Jardins de Alfabia, AA/K Paterson; **80** Orient, AA/C Sawyer; **80/81** Placa Major, Pollenca, AA/K Paterson; **82t** Port de Pollenca, AA/P Baker; **82b** Net repairs, Port de Soller, AA/P Baker; **83** Sa Calobra, AA/ P Baker; **84** Gorg Blau reservoir, AA/K Paterson; **86t** Sant Bartomeu Church, Soller, AA/K Paterson; **86b** Banco Central Hispano, Soller, AA/K Paterson; **87** Soller, AA/K Paterson; **88** Son Marriog, AA/K Paterson; **89** Arta from Sanctuary of St Salvador, AA/K Paterson; **90/91**Arta, AA/P Baker; **91** Sanctuary of St Salvador, AA/K Paterson; **92tr** Cala Millor, AA/P Baker; **92cr** Restaurant menu, AA/K Paterson; **93** Capdepera, AA/K Paterson; **94** Muro, AA/K Paterson; **95** Ethnology Museum, Muro, AA/K Paterson; **96** Track to Puig Maria Monastery, AA/J Cowham; **96/97** Punta d'en Amer, AA/P Baker; **98t** Parc Natural de S'Albufera, AA/C Sawyer; **98cr** Bird, Parc Natural de S'Albufera, AA/C Sawyer; **99** Ses Paises, AA/J Cowham; **100** Market, Santa Maria del Cami, AA/K Paterson; **102t** Car'n Gordiola, Algaida, AA/K Paterson; **102c** Window at Car'n Gordiola, Algaida, AA/K Paterson; **103** Cabrera Island, AA/C Sawyer; **104/105** Cala Figuera cove, AA/P Baker; **105tl** Fisherman, Cala Figuera, AA/K Paterson; **105cr** Statue, Campos, AA/P Baker; **106/107** Capocorb Vell, AA/K Paterson; **107** Colonia de Sant Jordi, AA/ P Baker; **109** Caves of Drac, AA/K Paterson; **110t** Ermita de Bonany, AA/P Baker; **110b** Sant Miguel Church, Felanitx, AA/K Paterson; **111** Leather factory, Inca, AA/P Baker; **112/113** Placa d'Espanya, Llucmajor, AA/K Paterson; **113** Pearl jewellery, Manacor, AA/K Paterson; **114l** Birthplace of Fran Junipero Serra, Petra, AA/J Cowham; **114r** Fran Junipero Serra, AA/K Paterson; **115** Platja de Palma, AA/P Baker; **116** Market in Porreres, AA/K Paterson; **116/117t** Sant Miguel Church, Felanitx, AA/K Paterson; **118/119** Porto Colom, AA/K Paterson; **119** Porto Cristo, AA/K Paterson; **120** Santuari de Cura, AA/P Baker; **120/121** Church, Puig de Randa, AA/K Paterson; **122** Window in Santanyi, AA/P Baker; **122/123** Santuari de Sant Salvador, AA/P Baker; **124** Botanicactus, AA/K Paterson; **125** Market, Sineu, AA/K Paterson; **126** Market, Vilafranca de Bonany, AA/K Paterson; **127** Ses Espigues restaurant, Valldemossa, AA/C Sawyer.

Every effort has been made to trace the copyright holders, and we apologise in advance for any accidental errors. We would be happy to apply the corrections in the following edition of this publication

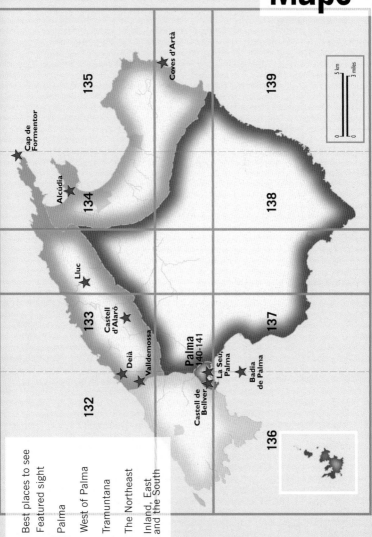

Cap de Formentor

Alcúdia

Coves d'Artà

Lluc

Castell d'Alaró

Deià

Valldemossa

Palma
140-141

La Seu, Palma

Castell de Bellver

Badia de Palma

133

135

134

132

139

138

137

136

Best places to see
★ Featured sight

☆ ■ Palma
☆ ■ West of Palma
☆ ■ Tramuntana
☆ ■ The Northeast
☆ ■ Inland, East and the South

5 km
3 miles

A

B

C

D

E

F

1   2   3   4

Na Foradada
Son Marroig
Miramar
87
Fonta
C710

Sa Marina
Port de Valldemossa
Son n'Olésa
Cala
Gata George
Son Coll   Sand
C710   Es Noguera
Nova Valldemossa
Banyalbufar
561m
C710   Claret
595m
Planícia   Moleta de Son Cabaspre
934m   Esporles
Planícia
La Granja   PM-112
Estellencs   893m
Puntals de   Ses Rogetes
Son Fortesa
1027m   PM-104
C710
928m   Son Espanyol
Esclop   Puig de Galatzó
483m   **La Reserva**   Puigpunyent   Establiments
  Galilea   Son Serralta   Establiments
Es Rafal   Vell
674m
Puig de na Baucà   Son Roca-
Son Ximelis
Sa Vileta
Parc Natural
de Sa Dragonera   *Cala en*
Basset   483m
349m   Puig de sa Grua
Es   **Sant**
Far Vell   **Elm**   PM-103   S'Arracó   Sa Comà
Es Pantaleu   361m   Castell
Font   de Bellver
312m   **136**
Sa Dragonera   Puig d'en Ric   **Andratx**   Es   486m   **Fundació Pilar**
Mont Port   Ses Egos   Capdellà   Puig Gros   **i Joan Miró**
C719   C719   **Calvià**   de Berdinat

Serra de Tramuntana

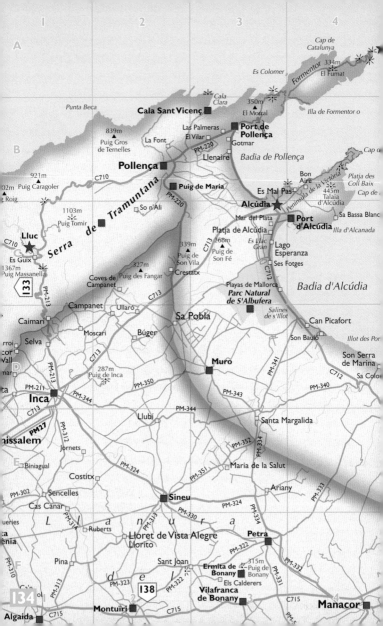

Cap de Formentor

s Pinar

enorca

Cap Ferrutx
432m
Talaia
de Moreia

Es Caló
Cala Mata
444m
Puig de sa
Tudossa

Cala Mata

Caló des
Corb Marí
Betlem
561m
Puig Morei

Cala
Torta
Platja de Sa
Mesquida
Cap des Freu
Escull des Freu

Estany del
Bisbe
S'Estanyol
Ermita de
Betlem

Cala
Mesquida
271m
Talaia de
Son Jaumell

Colònia
de Sant Pere

Cala Nau
Cala Lliteres
Punta de
Capdepera

Cala Rajada

Pare Natural
de la Península
de Llevant
522m
Puig de Ferrutx

Castell de Capdepera
Capdepera
Cala Moll

Son Fortesa
Vell

C715

Artà
Ses Païsses
Font de sa
Cala Provencal

C712
487m
Puig d'Alpare
Carrossa
Ses
Fulles

Coves d'Artà
Cap Vermell

473m
Muntanya
de Calicant
382m
Muntanya
Esquerda
Canyamel
Costa de
Canyamel
Platges de
Canyamel

Costa de
los Pinos
Cap des Pinar o des Raix

Sant Llorenç
des Cardassar
Son
Cervera
Port Nou
Port Verd

PM-403
271m
Puig de
sa Font
Cala Bona

Cala Millor

C715
184m
Puig de ses
Talaies
Son Moro Buenavista
Son Moro

Son Mas
Son Carrió
Auto-Safari
Punta de n'Amer

Platja de sa Coma
Cala Moreia
Platja de sa Moreia
Cala Morlanda

PM-402

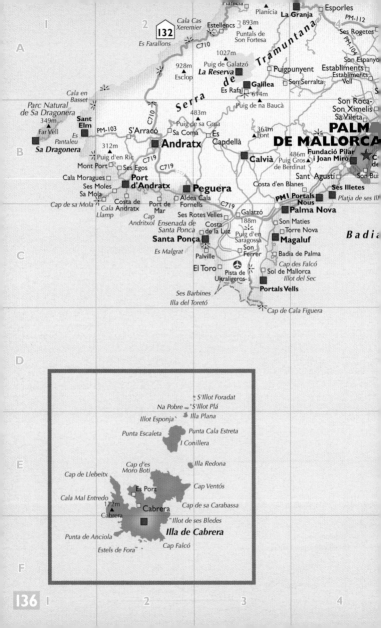

Palma de Mallorca

S'EIXAMPLE

CIUTAT ANTIGA

SA CALATRAVA

SA PORTELLA

Mercat Olivar

Museu d'Art
Espanyol
Contemporani

Fundació
La Caixa
(Gran Hotel)

Basílica de
Sant Francesc

Museu de
Mallorca

Banys
Àrabs

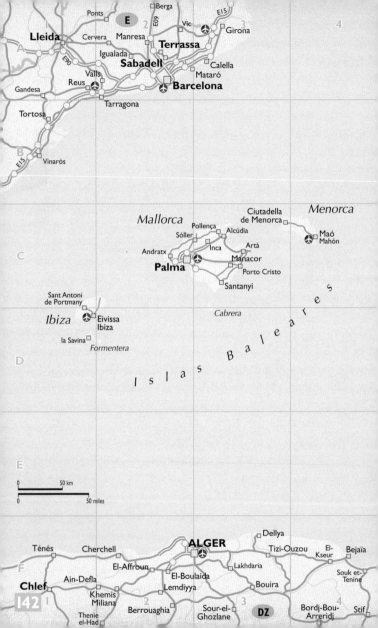

Ponts
Berga
E
E15
Vic
Girona
Lleida
Cervera
Manresa
E09
Terrassa
Igualada
Sabadell
Calella
Valls
Mataró
Gandesa
Reus
Barcelona
Tarragona
Tortosa
E15
Vinarós

Mallorca
Ciutadella
de Menorca
Menorca
Pollença
Sóller
Alcúdia
Maó
Mahón
Andratx
Inca
Artà
Palma
Manacor
Porto Cristo
Santanyi

Sant Antoni
de Portmany
Cabrera
Ibiza
Eivissa
Ibiza
la Savina
Formentera

Islas Baleares

50 km

50 miles

Dellya
ALGER
Ténés
Cherchell
Tizi-Ouzou
El-
Kseur
Bejaïa
El-Affroun
Lakhdaria
Souk et-
Tenine
Ain-Defla
El-Boulaida
Chlef
Lemdiyya
Bouira
Khemis
Miliana
Berrouaghia
Sour-el-
Ghozlane
Bordj-Bou-
Arreridj
Stif
Thenie
el-Had
DZ

142

Notes

Notes